More Weekends for Two in Northern California

50 Romantic Getaways

More Weekends for Two in Northern California

50 Romantic Getaways

Completely Revised and Updated

Second Edition

BY BILL GLEESON

PHOTOGRAPHS BY JOHN SWAIN

CHRONICLE BOOKS

SAN FRANCISCO

Contents

ACKNOWLEDGMENTS

Regina Miesch, photographic stylist
Yvonne Gleeson, research assistance
Ed and Susan Hepler
Michael and Nancy Finn
John and Debbie Lewis
Robert and Ferne Gleeson
Richard and Isabel Gomes
Kari and Jeff Gleeson

Text copyright © 2000 by Bill Gleeson
Photographs/Illustrations copyright © 2000 by John Swain
Library of Congress Cataloging-in-Publication Data
available.

ISBN 0-8118-2626-0

Printed in Hong Kong.

Typesetting by Jaime Robles

Distributed in Canada by Raincoast Books
8680 Cambie Street
Vancouver, British Columbia V6P 6M9

10 9 8 7 6 5 4 3 2 1

Chronicle Books
85 Second Street
San Francisco, California 94105

www.chroniclebooks.com

Introduction

*I*f you've ever visited an ice cream parlor and agonized over the menu of flavors, you'll have some appreciation of the bittersweet decisions that faced us in creating the original edition of *Weekends for Two in Northern California*. In a region that encompasses some of the world's most coveted romantic destinations, narrowing a listing to only fifty was overwhelming.

Fortunately, that first volume struck a chord among traveling romantics and spawned a still-expanding series of *Weekends for Two* guides—seven at this writing. In between searching out romantic destinations in other parts of the country, we were invited to produce a Northern California sequel.

This revised edition of *More Weekends for Two in Northern California* spotlights fifty wonderfully seductive inns and small hotels, each chosen to further expand your romantic travel horizons. In assembling and updating this book, we were guided by our original goal: to take the guess-work out of planning a special getaway and to help ensure that your experience is a memorable one—for all the right reasons.

Rooms for Romance

When evaluating the romantic potential of inns and small hotels, we look for a certain ambience as well as specific features that engender romance. Our checklist includes:

- Private bathrooms (we name any rooms that share)
- In-room fireplaces
- Tubs or showers big enough for two
- Breakfast in bed or in your room
- Feather beds and cushy comforters
- Canopied, four-poster, king-sized beds
- Couches, love seats, or nooks for sitting together
- Private decks, patios, or balconies with inspirational views
- Romantic decor, special touches, and thoughtful accessories

Few destinations offer this complete menu of niceties, but each must offer at least some of these features. We also seek out hotels and inns that exude that overall, sometimes difficult-to-describe, intimate atmosphere and those that discourage child guests, since many dedicated moms and dads are seeking a well-deserved break from the kids.

Finally, we avoid destinations referred to in the lodging industry as homestays. These are private homes in which a room or rooms are rented out to travelers, often—as we have discovered from experience—by owners lacking skill in the art of innkeeping.

Within the inns and small hotels listed in this book, we discovered special rooms that are particularly conducive to a romantic experience. Instead of leaving the choice of rooms to the reservation clerk and describing in detail the public areas of each establishment, we've devoted a good part of this book to details of particularly romantic rooms and suites. When booking your getaway reservation, don't hesitate to ask about the availability of a specific room—unless, of course, you already have a personal favorite.

Tables for Two

At the beginning of each regional listing, we've identified particularly noteworthy restaurants near our featured destinations. These were sampled by us and/or recommended by innkeepers whose opinions we respect. Keep in mind, however, that restaurants—and chefs—come and go. Accordingly, we suggest that you balance these recommendations with updates and new choices offered by your innkeepers. We also recommend that you make reservations for dinner well before your departure date.

Your Favorites

If we've overlooked one of your cherished romantic destinations in our two volumes of *Weekends for Two in Northern California,* you may contact us by U.S. mail (see address below), by e-mail at weekends42@aol.com, or check the Chronicle Books Web site at www.chroniclebooks.com. We look forward to sharing new romantic weekends for two in future printings.

A Word About Rates

Travelers scouting the highways for discount lodgings can still find a no-frills motel room for under $50. However, these guides aren't for bargain hunters. We view your romantic times together as the most special of occasions, and through years of travel we've confirmed the adage, you get what you pay for. Consequently, we've come to expect that a special room commands a higher price. In fact, you'll find that few rooms described in these pages cost less than $100 per night.

To help you plan your getaway budget, approximate 2000 rates for specific rooms are noted within each description. Keep in mind that an increasing number of establishments require two-night minimum stays on weekends and holidays.

Rates are classified at the end of each listing in the following ranges, not including tax:

Moderate: Under $150
Expensive: $150–$200
Deluxe: Over $200

Final Notes

No payment was sought or accepted from any establishment in exchange for a listing in this book.

Food, wine, and flowers were often added to our photo scenes for styling purposes. Some inns provide these amenities; others do not. Please ask when making a reservation whether these items are complimentary or whether they're provided for an extra charge.

We hope our readers understand that there's no guarantee that these properties will maintain furnishings or standards as they existed on our visit, and we very much appreciate hearing from readers if their experience is at variance with our descriptions. Reader comments are carefully consulted in the creation and revision of each *Weekends for Two* volume. Your opinions are critical, and we share reader raves and criticisms (anonymously) in occasional travel updates that are available free of charge by sending a stamped, self-addressed envelope to Bill Gleeson, Weekends for Two, P.O. Box 6324, Folsom, CA 95763.

The North Coast

DAYTIME DIVERSIONS

Salt Point State Park and Kruse Rhododendron Reserve near Timberhill Ranch offer six thousand acres of trails that extend to the ocean. Timberhill's own eighty acres offer hiking opportunities as well. Just north of Mendocino, in Russian Gulch State Park, an easy six-and-a-half-mile hike will bring you to a romantic waterfall. At day's end, savor the sunset from Mendocino Headlands State Park on Little Lake Road.

Our favorite north coast galleries include Alinder (photography) and Woodbridge, both on Highway 1 in Gualala, and Henley's, just off Highway 1 on Annapolis Road at the Sea Ranch.

From its base in Fort Bragg, the Skunk Line conducts vintage rail excursions through towering redwoods.

TABLES FOR TWO

In Gualala, you'll enjoy the romantic dining room at St. Orres (see separate listing in this section) or the Old Milano Hotel, both located on Highway 1. From personal experience, we can also recommend the multicourse dinners served to guests and the general public high on a coastal ridge at Timberhill Ranch in Cazadero (see separate listing in this section).

Cafe Beaujolais (961 Ukiah) and the restaurant called 955 Ukiah are the culinary icons of Mendocino. Call well in advance for reservations. Just south of Mendocino, Stevenswood (Highway 1 in Little River) and the Albion River Inn (Highway 1 in Albion) have standout restaurants.

Restaurant 301 at the Hotel Carter in Eureka (see Bell Cottage and Carter Cottage in this section) has received high praise for its food and for its extensive wine cellar.

TIMBERHILL RANCH

35755 Hauser Bridge Road
Cazadero, CA 95421
Telephone: (707) 847-3258

Fifteen cottages, each with private bath, deck, and woodburning fireplace. No telephones or televisions in cottages. Amenities include bathrobes, small refrigerators, and stereo systems. Operates on modified American plan (continental breakfast and dinner included). Breakfast is delivered to your cottage. Swimming pool, spa, and tennis courts. Smoking permitted in certain cottages only. Disabled access. Two-night minimum stay on weekends; three-night minimum stay during holiday periods. Deluxe.

Getting There
From Highway 1, ninety miles north of San Francisco and five miles north of Jenner, turn right on Meyers Grade Road and follow for thirteen-and-a-half miles to ranch. (Note: Meyers Grade Road becomes Seaview Road, which later turns into Hauser Bridge Road.)

Timberhill Ranch

Cazadero

*C*ontrary to the images that its name might conjure, Timberhill Ranch isn't a rustic retreat for burly lumberjacks or a dusty cattle spread. This is one of the most sumptuous romantic hideaways we've discovered along the North Coast.

This intimate resort, set high on a coastal ridge about one mile from the ocean, had its beginnings as a ranch and later as an alternative high school. The mid-1980s brought new ownership and several freestanding guest cottages that now comprise the small country inn resort. My partner likened Timberhill to a luxurious summer camp for adults.

Rooms for Romance

Our home for a night, Cottage 14, is typical of Timberhill's accommodations. The large one-room cottage, with cedar log-style paneling, holds a queen-sized bed, an armoire, two cushy chairs, and a table and chairs set. An expertly built fire awaited only a match. The spacious and contemporary separate bathroom is equipped with double sinks and a large shower with double seats.

Each Timberhill cottage is situated so as to provide optimal privacy. Our expansive, side-facing deck offered wonderful views of nature without exposing other cabins. Cars aren't allowed within the compound and cottages are reached via winding gravel pathways. Electric carts tote guest luggage between cottages and the parking area.

Cottages 8, 9, and 10, which face a large pond, are the most oft-requested. Cottages 9 and 10 receive the most sun. Cottages 3 and 5 also afford nice pond views.

A walking trail leads from the ranch to a small, romantic cliff-side deck overlooking the ocean—perfect for a picnic lunch.

Dinners at Timberhill are served in a beautiful open dining room whose many windows afford panoramic mountain vistas. An adjacent building houses the reception and parlor areas. There's also a common area with satellite television and a large swimming pool, and a spa on-site.

Per-night rates at Timberhill, which include continental breakfast and six-course dinner for two, are in the high $300 range. Midweek rates are less. There's also a charge of around $20 if you request a specific cottage.

North Coast travelers should be aware that Timberhill Ranch isn't an ocean-view property, nor is it a destination that will appeal to folks looking for shopping or nightlife. However, for those who savor solitude, and romantic enchantment in an unspoiled natural setting, it doesn't get any better.

St. Orres

36601 South Highway 1
Gualala, CA 95445
Telephone: (707) 884-3303

Thirteen cottage units with private bath; most with fireplaces or woodburning stoves; some with tubs for two. Complimentary full breakfast served in the inn's restaurant or in your room. Restaurant serves fixed-price dinners. Spa. No disabled access. Two-night minimum stay on weekends; three-night minimum stay during holiday periods. Smoking is allowed in cottages. Moderate to expensive.

Getting There
From Highway 101 at Petaluma, exit at Washington Street and drive west through town toward the coast. At Highway 1, turn north and follow to Gualala. Inn is two miles north of town on right. From Highway 101 at Santa Rosa, exit at River Road (becomes Highway 116) and drive west toward the coast. At Highway 1 south of Jenner, turn north and follow to Gualala. Inn is two miles north of town on right. Check in at the main building. The innkeeper will provide you with a map to your cottage.

St. Orres

Gualala

*T*he artful Russian-style domes and weathered redwood facade of St. Orres are a familiar sight to motorists passing through Gualala on coastal Highway 1. Unbeknownst to many travelers, however, is the collection of romantic cottages that are all but hidden from view among the trees behind the main building. So remote are these jewels that you'll have to get back in the car and drive to your cottage after checking in at the registration desk.

Rooms for Romance

The hand-crafted cottages at St. Orres are clustered in two areas. The Meadows, located up-slope from the main building, consists of four cottages. Our favorite here is Tree House (around $200), a remote retreat that oozes romance. Guests have an ocean view from the private deck, from the couch in the separate sitting area, and from the queen-sized bed. In the tiled bathroom we discovered a deep soaking tub for two. Tree House

also boasts a woodburning stove, a wet bar, lots of windows, and a large skylight.

Rose Cottage (mid $100 range), which offers the best ocean view, has an elevated bedroom and a sitting area furnished with a woodburning stove and sofa bed. Guest House (low $100 range) has a cozy window seat, a woodburning stove, and a private deck overlooking a meadow.

The rustic Wildflower Cottage (around $100) has a loft with a double bed, a woodburning stove, and a seductive outdoor hot water shower with a forest view.

Just north of the main building is the other compound, called Creekside, where guests have use of a facility equipped with a spa, sauna, and sun deck. Eight cottages dot the forested grounds here.

Two popular Creekside cottages are Pine Haven (around $200) and Sequoia (around $200). Pine Haven borrows its distinctive architecture from the Russian-style main building. Inside the spacious, two-bedroom, domed cottage is a tiled breakfast area with an ocean view, an attractive woodburning fireplace, and a wet bar. There are two redwood decks.

Sequoia, the resort's most oft-requested cottage (around $200), contains an elevated bedroom alcove illuminated by a skylight. The bathroom holds a deep soaking tub for two. You'll also be treated to an ocean view and a spacious deck.

Offered for around $100 at the time of our visit, the rustic and simple Fern Canyon is one of the north coast's best romantic bargains. This cozy cottage, equipped with a double bed, also features two redwood decks.

In addition to a superb restaurant that is open to the public, the main building at St. Orres holds eight small upstairs rooms that share bathrooms. We do not recommend these accommodations for romantic getaways.

North Coast Country Inn

34591 South Highway 1
Gualala, CA 95445
Telephone: (707) 884-4537 or
toll-free: (800) 959-4537

Six rooms, each with private bath, woodburning or gas fireplace, kitchenette, and deck. Complimentary full breakfast served in common room. Spa. No disabled access. Smoking is not permitted. Two-night minimum stay required during weekends; three-night minimum stay required during holiday periods. Moderate.

Getting There
From Highway 101 at Petaluma, exit at Washington Street and drive west through town toward the coast. At Highway 1, turn north and follow to Gualala. Inn is four miles north of town. From Highway 101 at Santa Rosa, exit at River Road, which becomes Highway 116, and drive west toward the coast. At Highway 1 south of Jenner, turn north and follow to Gualala. Inn is four miles north of town on right.

North Coast Country Inn

Gualala

*A*fter visits to the seductive Seacliff and Whale Watch Inn for our first volume of *Weekends for Two*, and more recently to St. Orres, we were fairly convinced that we had exhausted the romantic potential of tiny Gualala (pronounced wa-LA-la). Then we happened upon Loren and Nancy Flanagan's enchanting North Coast Country Inn north of town and concluded that, with all due respect to Mendocino, Gualala is the north coast's most romantic village.

This weathered, redwood-sided inn, nearly hidden behind lush foliage on the east side of

Highway 1, is a real charmer, boasting a definite pride of ownership. Converted in the mid-1980s from an art gallery, it overlooks the ocean and is within ear shot of a convivial sea lion rookery. The playful barking in the distance is but one of the inn's appealing characteristics.

Rooms for Romance

Each of the inn's six rooms, offered in the mid to upper $100 range, is a winner, but we have our own favorites. New since our first visit is Forest House, whose upper level boasts the inn's two most opulent accommodations, both offered in the upper $100 range. In Southwind, equipped with a king-sized brass bed, a fireplace, and a whirlpool tub, the two of you will be treated to a lovely southerly view of the coastline. Next door, the pine-paneled Evergreen overlooks a hillside garden, and also has a fireplace and a whirlpool tub. Breakfast and evening refreshments are served in the common area that comprises the first level of Forest House.

Gallery (mid $100 range) has long been a favorite among honeymooners. French doors open to a very private retreat with a skylit, queen-sized, four-poster bed, a gas fireplace, and a wet bar. A sheltered private deck out front can be enjoyed year-round. Traveling romantics should note that this room does not offer an ocean view.

Also among our favorite rooms is Sea Urchin (mid $100 range), a large bright corner room with a vine-draped side deck. This room, which offers just a peek of ocean, is equipped with two comfortable chairs, a handcrafted tester bed, a brick fireplace, and a kitchenette. Above is an open-beamed ceiling with exposed wooden trusses. The adjacent Quilt and Aquitaine rooms are similarly equipped and have filtered ocean views.

A romantic bonus are two lovely retreats maintained on the upper part of the inn's property. One wooded path leads up a hillside to a secluded hot tub under the trees, while another trail ends at a little glen with a quaint gazebo and sitting deck.

Wharfmaster's Inn

785 Port Road
Point Arena, CA 95468
Telephone: (707) 882-3171 or
toll free: (800) 932-4031

Twenty-four rooms, each with private bath and tub for two; twenty-two rooms with fireplaces. Amenities include complimentary bottle of local wine. Disabled access. Smoking is not allowed. Two-night minimum stay required during holiday periods. Moderate to expensive.

Getting There
From Highway 101 four miles north of Santa Rosa, exit at River Road and drive west for twenty-seven miles to Jenner. Head north on Highway 1 and drive sixty miles to Point Arena. Turn left on Iverson Road (turns into Port Road) and drive one and a half miles to inn. Point Arena is one hundred forty miles north of San Francisco and one hundred sixty miles from Sacramento.

Wharfmaster's Inn

Point Arena Cove

*I*n the mid-1880s, an ornate, eastlake-style Victorian home was built on a hillside overlooking the sea for the wharfmaster of the Point Arena Cove. Today the landmark residence is the centerpiece of Wharfmaster's Inn, one of the secret romantic retreats we discovered along the rugged Mendocino coast.

A cluster of contemporary-style, two-story buildings, each painted brown with white trim, sit adjacent to and above the original home, whose interior is pictured here. Some of the inn's rooms, offered in the low $100 range, offer hillside and/or courtyard views; others, priced from the mid $100 range and up, offer dramatic ocean vistas.

Rooms for Romance

The renovated former home of the wharfmaster's family now boasts luxury accommodations that can sleep two to four couples.

A two-room suite here (low $200 range), which can be closed off from the rest of the house, has a tiny bathroom placed between the bedroom and sitting room. The bedroom features an antique bed covered with a lush, cream-colored spread, while the sitting room contains a large whirlpool tub for two surrounded by tile and mirrors. Doors open onto an oceanside deck.

The Lookout wing offers spectacular ocean views. Lookout Room C, for example, has a queen-sized four-poster bed placed beside a glass door and ocean-view deck. With rose-colored carpet, dried flowers, and antiques, the room's interior strikes a pleasant contrast to the rustic facade. There's no reason to stray farther than the four walls here. Simply light a fire, open the door, lie back in the whirlpool tub for two, and listen to the ever present sound of the surf.

Just below the hillside inn is a commercial building that, at the time of our visit, housed a pizza parlor and a seafood restaurant.

Fensalden Inn

33810 Navarro Ridge Road
Albion, CA 95410
Telephone: (707) 937-4042 or
toll-free: (800) 959-3850

Eight rooms, each with private bath; all with fire-places. Complimentary full breakfast served at communal table. Complimentary appetizers served each afternoon. Disabled access. Smoking is not permitted. Two-night minimum stay required during weekends; three-night minimum stay required during holiday periods. Moderate to expensive.

Getting There
From Highway 101 at Cloverdale, drive west on Highway 128 toward the coast. At Highway 1, turn north and drive two miles to Navarro Ridge Road. Turn right and drive one-quarter of a mile to inn on left.

Fensalden Inn

Albion

*T*he years have been kind to stately Fensalden, a former way station and tavern where stagecoach passengers traveling between Northern California's coastal and valley communities cooled their heels over a hundred years ago. Evidence of shotgun blasts in the sturdy, hundred-year-old ceiling attests to the intemperate goings on during the old days when Albion was a remote outpost.

Fortunately, it's much calmer here these days, the coastal quiet interrupted only by whispering couples and flickering fires.

Rooms for Romance

Of the five homespun rooms within the handsome main house, we recommend the second-floor Hawthorne Suite (mid $100 range), a spacious love nest tucked under the eaves with a separate sitting room and a sleeping room with a queen-sized canopy bed and a fireplace. The east and west views include open pasture lands that sweep to the ocean.

An enclosed antique water tower holds two other charming rooms. The Tower Room (mid $100 range) has a cathedral ceiling and a corner brick fireplace. Three tall windows overlook cypress trees that frame an ocean view.

The most unusual accommodation on the property is the Bungalow (around $200) situated a few hundred yards from the main house. Resembling a relic from the psychedelic sixties, this eclectic, freestanding hideaway features lots of intriguing angles, big wooden beams, and windows. It's equipped with two queen-sized beds, a love seat facing a gas fireplace, and a private bathroom with a spa tub and a separate shower. There are also two lofts, each with a twin-sized bed. The full kitchen features a redwood burl countertop. If you enjoy a rustic environment and are open to a different overnight experience, you'll get a kick out of the Bungalow. If your tastes are more traditional, you probably won't.

A mowed path through Fensalden's twenty acres offers soothing ocean vistas.

Agate Cove Bed-and-Breakfast Inn

11201 Lansing Street
Mendocino, CA 95460
Telephone: (707) 937-0551

Ten rooms, each with private bath; nine with fire-places and two with tubs for two. Amenities include morning newspaper brought to your door. Complimentary full breakfast served at communal tables. Smoking is not permitted. Two-night mini-mum stay required during weekends; three-night minimum stay required during holiday periods. Moderate to expensive.

Getting There
From northbound Highway 1 in Mendocino, turn left at Lansing Street (third exit in town) and follow to inn driveway on left.

Agate Cove Bed-and-Breakfast Inn

Mendocino

*C*harming cottages overlooking the churning Pacific, white Adirondack chairs on the lawn facing the water, beautiful sunsets, fireplaces to warm your toes... Agate Cove is quintessential Mendocino.

Consisting primarily of quaint blue-and-white cottages (some of them are duplex units) with simple but comfortable furnishings, the inn occupies a gentle hill just a stone's throw from the ocean cliffs. The white-water and blue-water views from this property are among the most dramatic we've found.

Rooms for Romance

We have four favorite cottages. The best of the bunch are Emerald and Obsidian (mid $200 range), whose picture windows and outdoor decks have dramatic views of the Mendocino headlands and the ocean. These also have nicely dressed, king-sized four-poster beds, fireplaces, and in the bathrooms, huge tubs for two (with bubble bath) that double as spacious showers with his and hers spigots.

Garnet and Topaz (mid to upper $100 range) are situated off by themselves and are simi-

larly furnished with king-sized four-poster beds and fireplaces. These cottages, which also afford good ocean views, are equipped with showers for two.

The property is situated between Highway 1 and the ocean cliffs, and the sound of traffic can be heard. Agate Cove was sold since our first visit, and the new owners were adding a sound wall when we dropped by for a return visit. The Zircon, Moonstone, and Topaz cottages back up to the highway. The Garden room has neither an ocean view nor outside seating.

A grand breakfast, cooked on a wood-burning stove, is served at communal tables in a stunning picture-windowed breakfast room in the inn's main building.

REED MANOR

Palette Drive
Mendocino, CA 95460
Telephone: (707) 937-5446

Five rooms, each with private bath, gas fireplace,
tub for two, television with videocassette player,
stereo radio, refrigerator, and telephone with
answering machine. Complimentary continental
breakfast placed in your room's refrigerator prior to
check-in. No disabled access. Smoking is not permitted indoors. Two-night minimum stay required
on weekends; three-night minimum stay during holiday periods. Expensive to deluxe.

Getting There
From northbound Highway 1 in Mendocino, turn
left on Little Lake Road. Turn right on Lansing
Street and right on Palette Drive to inn driveway on
right.

Reed Manor

Mendocino

*I*n a laid-back community where homespun country inns are de rigueur, Reed Manor is an anomaly. Without question Mendocino's premier luxury inn, the Manor tempts guests with the ultimate in romantic splendor.

Commanding a lofty hillside perch overlooking the village, Reed Manor is a contemporary-style retreat that resembles a grand residence.

Rooms for Romance

If your heart is set on an ocean view, only the second-floor Napoleon or Majestic Rose will do. In our opinion, Napoleon is the most romantic guest room in Mendocino. This elegant hideaway offers a canopied king-sized bed and a small covered balcony overlooking the village and ocean. A two-sided gas fireplace is visible from the bedroom as well as from the seductive bathroom, which contains an oval tub for two and a spacious shower with a vertical set of water jets. There's also a television in the bathroom. Although this room carries a hefty rate of around $300 per night, it has all the ingredients for a romantic experience you'll not soon forget.

Next door is Majestic Rose, a two-room suite fit for a king, and carrying a king-sized rate (in the mid $400 range).

The least expensive room in the manor (upper $100 range) is Imperial Garden, a comparatively small room that exudes a somewhat formal ambience. Guests here have a private elevated outdoor deck (no ocean view).

Morning Glory, one of the inn's most popular rooms, attracts the morning sun and carries a rate in the mid $200 range. The centerpiece here is an oval-shaped spa tub that can be curtained off from the rest of the room, if desired. The private deck is equipped with a high-powered telescope for village viewing.

Josephine's Garden (around $200) is a tastefully wallpapered, first-floor end unit with a spacious outdoor deck (no ocean view).

BELL COTTAGE AND CARTER COTTAGE

301 L Street (check-in address)
Eureka, CA 95501
Telephone: (707) 444-8062

Three-room cottage and one-room cottage, each
with private bath, spa tub for two, and television
with videocassette player and video library; three
with fireplaces. Complimentary full breakfast served
in the Hotel Carter. Complimentary tea, cookies,
and wine. Restaurant. No disabled access. Smoking
is not permitted. Two-night minimum stay required
during weekends and holiday periods. Moderate to
expensive.

Getting There
From Highway 101 in downtown Eureka, drive west
on L Street through Old Town and check in at
Hotel Carter, Third and L streets.

Bell Cottage and Carter Cottage

Eureka

*I*nnkeeper Mark Carter continues to entice traveling romantics to the north coastal burg of Eureka with an expanding array of romantic accommodations. Obviously not satisfied with the ornate manse and Victorian-style hotel featured in our original book, Mark and his wife, Christi, have done it again with the addition of two sumptuous cottages to the Carter compound. The single-story, yellow-and-white Bell Cottage sits near the Carter House mansion country inn that Mark personally handcrafted some years back. More recently, Carter Cottage, a honeymoon-quality hideaway, opened right next door.

Bell Cottage

The exterior is nineteenth-century Victorian, but Bell Cottage's interior boasts contemporary conveniences that the original residents couldn't have even dreamed about. There are only three rooms in the inn, and each is trimmed with rich woods and marble. Bathrooms are equipped marble-faced spa tubs for two. Fine modern art decorates the walls, and all rooms have CD players and televisions.

Rooms 1 and 3 (low to mid $200 range) have woodburning fireplaces and queen-sized beds, while Room 2 (mid to upper $100 range), a somewhat smaller retreat, holds a double bed. There's also a common parlor with a fireplace and a contemporary kitchen available for guest use.

Carter Cottage

Perhaps the most romantic of the Carter array, Carter Cottage, decorated in bright, sunny colors, holds a deep marble spa tub, fireplaces in both the sleeping and living areas, and a private deck offering Humboldt Bay views.

What makes a night here truly special becomes evident in the evening when a team of culinary experts drops by to create a custom-tailored, multicourse dinner for two in the cottage's fully equipped demonstration kitchen. The price, including dinner, is around $500.

Guests staying at either cottage are treated to a multicourse breakfast, wine and hors d'oeuvres in the evening, and cookies and tea at bedtime.

The Wine Country

DAYTIME DIVERSIONS

The art of winemaking complements an impressive exhibition of contemporary art at the Hess Collection winery. You'll enjoy the woodsy drive west from Napa along Redwood Road into the mountains to this unusual backroad winery and gallery.

Napa Valley picnic fixings may be purchased at Oakville Grocery on Highway 29 in Oakville. Then head west on Oakville Grade a short distance to Vichon Winery, site of one of the valley's preeminent picnic spots. Don't forget to first obtain permission at the tasting room to use a table.

Among the dozen or so spas in quaint Calistoga is Indian Springs Spa and Resort, in operation for more than a century. It offers mud and mineral baths and massages, as well as use of its heated outdoor swimming pool.

Call ahead to Jordan Vineyard and Winery outside Healdsburg (707-431-5250) and make an appointment to visit this impressive Bordeaux-style chateau and premium wine-making facility. Other Sonoma area wineries worth a visit include Hop Kiln and Buena Vista.

TABLES FOR TWO

Heirloom (110 West Spain Street, Sonoma) has received high praise since its 1999 opening. Another Sonoma winner is Della Santina's (133 East Napa Street). Applewood (described in this section) boasts a beautiful new dining room that serves multicourse, candlelit meals. We and our innkeepers also recommend Tre Scalini (241 Healdsburg Avenue), just off the plaza in Healdsburg; Calistoga Inn (1250 Lincoln Avenue, Calistoga); Showley's at Miramonte (1327 Railroad Avenue, St. Helena); and Terra (1345 Railroad Avenue, St. Helena). For a more casual experience, drop by Tomatina (1020 Main Street, St. Helena). Our Napa Valley favorites also include Tra Vigne (1050 Charter Oak at Highway 29, St. Helena). Tra Vigne's deli, Cantinetta, serves great take-out food.

AFTER HOURS

Savor the valley view with a glass of wine from the hillside terrace of Auberge du Soleil above the Silverado Trail in Rutherford. It doesn't get much more romantic than this.

CHURCHILL MANOR

485 Brown Street
Napa, CA 94559
Telephone: (707) 253-7733

Ten rooms, each with private bath and telephone;
five with fireplaces and large soaking tubs for two.
Complimentary full breakfast served in dining room
at tables for two or four, or taken to your room.
Complimentary evening wine and cheese and afternoon cookies served daily. Tandem bicycles available for free guest use. Disabled access. Smoking is
not permitted. Guests staying on a Saturday night
must stay a second night. Moderate to deluxe.

Getting There
From Highway 29, exit at First Street and follow
downtown Napa signs onto Second Street. Turn
right on Jefferson Street (first stoplight) and drive
two blocks to Oak Street. Turn left on Oak and
drive seven blocks to Brown Street. The inn is on
the southwest corner of Oak and Brown streets.

Churchill Manor

Napa

*B*rown Street, which runs through a quiet residential area of Napa, is home to two of our favorite Wine Country bed-and-breakfast inns. Occupying a lushly landscaped acre, the century-old Churchill Manor is as impressive an example of Second Empire style as you're likely to find anywhere in these parts. You'll fall in love with this stately manse the moment you walk through the garden and step up to the Southern-style veranda that sweeps around the front of the home. It's no wonder that hundreds of couples have recited their wedding vows here.

Rooms for Romance

Since our first visit, the owners have made many improvements to the inn. The spacious Edward Churchill room, which recently underwent a costly makeover, is an antique lover's dream, furnished with a matching antique French bedroom set consisting of an ornate king-sized bed, a triple-mirrored carved amoire, and marble-topped nightstands, dresser, and dressing table. The room's original fireplace is framed with gold leaf tiles. There's also a large pedestal bathtub in the bedroom and a tiled two-person shower in the bathroom. Offered in the low $200 range, this is one of the most romantic of the inn's ten rooms.

The third-floor Mary Wilder Room (around $200) also has been extensively remodeled, and is furnished with a king-sized bed, an ornate French armoire, and a gas fireplace. The bathroom beckons romantics with not only a large two-person shower but an oversized claw-foot tub.

Two other romantic choices are Victoria's Room and Rose's Room (high $100 range), which both feature impressive antique furnishings, oversized clawfoot tubs, and fireplaces in the sleeping rooms. There are separate showers in each of the bathrooms.

Half of the inn's rooms are located on the cozy and quiet third floor; most of these carry very reasonable rates in the mid $100 range. Among these, Amy's Room has a queen-sized brass bed, seating for the two of you, and a bathroom containing a tiled, two-person shower with stained glass accents.

Travelers should be aware that wedding parties frequently book the entire inn during week-end periods from the spring through the fall.

BLUE VIOLET MANSION

443 Brown Street
Napa, CA 94559
Telephone: (707) 253-2583 or
toll-free: (800) 959-2583

Seventeen rooms, each with private bath; most with
gas fireplaces; eleven with tubs for two. Full
gourmet breakfast can be taken at a communal table
or in your room. Innkeepers serve private, gourmet,
multicourse dinners in your room at extra charge.
Candlelit dinners for two (at around $150) also
served nightly in the grand salon. Swimming pool
and spa. Disabled access. Smoking is not permitted.
Two-night minimum stay required during weekends
from February through November and holiday periods. Expensive to deluxe.

Getting There
From Highway 29 in Napa, exit east at First Street.
Turn right on California Street and drive three
blocks to Oak Street. Turn left and drive one-half
mile to Brown Street. Turn right on Brown Street.

Blue Violet Mansion

Napa

*J*n Napa, the quality of older homes-turned-inns is as diverse as the region's wines, from the inexpensive generics to aging beauties waiting to be savored. Tucked away among other architectural gems and just a short walk from downtown Napa, Blue Violet Mansion is, in our opinion, the cabernet of Napa's Victorian bed-and-breakfast inns.

This hundred-year-old gem had been operated as a chopped-up apartment building before Bob and Kathy Morris bought the home and began an immaculate restoration in 1990. After rehabilitating the structure the innkeepers filled the public and guest rooms with a trove of exquisite furnishings ranging from Victorian to contemporary pieces. Bob, an art collector, has lavished every room with tasteful prints, paintings, and sculpture. A whimsical fantasy theme, carried by unicorns, sorcerers, and griffins, is also evident in the public and guest rooms.

Rooms for Romance

Since we first discovered Blue Violet Mansion a few years ago, the inn has doubled in size, providing traveling romantics with an expanded array of romantic getaway options. Although there's not a bad room in the house, you'll be most tempted by the new Camelot theme rooms hidden away under the eaves high on the third floor. These four romantic retreats celebrate Old World England where, according to the innkeepers, "men were brave kings and knights who protected and adored their ladies."

The theme rooms are handpainted in trompe l'oeil style and feature two-person spa tubs, deluxe linens, fancy goblets, gas fireplaces, and CD players. The largest and most expensive of these is the Royal Suite (low $300 range), which offers a dormered sitting area. The coffered ceiling above the king-sized bed is painted to depict a night sky and also boasts lighted stained glass. There's a separate shower in the bathroom.

Priced in the mid $200 range on this floor is the Courtyard Garden Room, where a white pine queen-sized canopy bed serves as a romantic centerpiece. Dormer windows near the fireplace look out over Napa.

Chinese carpet covers the polished plank floor of His Majesty's Room (around $300), a beautiful second-floor retreat with a gas fireplace and an open bay window sitting area boasting a pleasant view of neighboring homes. A whirlpool spa tub for two with brass shower fixtures and granite floor await behind the bathroom door.

The Duchess' Parlor (around $200) is a spacious first-floor room that looks out onto redwood trees. The room, with a gas fireplace and sitting area, is furnished with a king-sized brass bed and lots of intriguing art and books. The bathroom has a large shower for two.

The inn's least expensive accommodation is Anastasia's Room (mid to upper $100 range), which has a corner gas fireplace, a queen-sized bed, and a bathroom with a shower for two.

La Residence Country Inn

4066 St. Helena Highway North
Napa, CA 94558
Telephone: (707) 253-0337

Twenty rooms, each with private bath. Sixteen rooms have woodburning fireplaces and three rooms have soaking tubs for two. Complimentary full breakfast served at tables for two in dining room. Swimming pool and spa. Disabled access. Smoking is not permitted. Two-night minimum stay during weekends; three-night minimum stay during holiday periods. Expensive to deluxe.

Getting There
From Highway 29 in Napa, drive north and turn right at the first opportunity after the Salvador Avenue traffic light. The Don Giovanni restaurant is on this corner. Make another right turn on the drive into the property and follow signs for parking and registration.

La Residence Country Inn

*Y*ou may not be familiar with this luxurious small inn, but if you travel Highway 29 out of Napa, it's right under your nose.

Tucked among oak trees and gardens along the highway just north of town, La Residence Country Inn offers guests a choice of either something old or something new, with each option served up with charm and taste. The centerpiece of the two-acre property is a contemporary, two-story, shingled building affectionately referred to as "the barn." Eleven guest rooms and dining facilities comprise the white-trimmed building. A short stroll away is the other half of the inn: an 1870 gothic-revival mansion built for a riverboat captain. The home holds nine rooms and suites.

A major landscaping effort undertaken since our first visit brought a park-like appearance to La Residence. The grounds now boast new lawn areas, gardens, and two ponds.

Rooms for Romance
The most popular room among romantics in-the-know is Room 22 (around $200) in the main building. Decorated in country style, this second-floor room has a brick woodburning fireplace that's visible from the queen-sized four-poster bed. Two sets of French doors open to a shared balcony. This and the other rooms have bathrooms with tiled tubs and showers.

A grand old oak tree stands just outside the window of Room 25, which holds a queen-sized brass bed. Room 21, accessed via a second-floor deck entry, features a spacious shower built for two in a skylit bathroom.

Rooms 12, 23, and 26 in the main building have deep soaking tubs for two. All rooms in this building feature French and English pine antiques. Double walls between guest rooms and three feet of space between floors ensure your privacy. However, some road noise can be heard.

Rooms in the mansion are spread over three floors and offer a more remote feeling, since they're away from the property's hub. All are furnished with walnut and oak antiques.

Room 31 (mid $200 range), a downstairs corner, is equipped with an antique fireplace, a couch, and a queen-sized four-poster bed. In the modern bathroom is a deep tub for two with shower.

Room 36, a second-floor suite, is decorated in rose tones and has a sitting room as well as a balcony with chairs. On the third floor are two rooms, each with a private bath.

Oak Knoll Inn

2200 East Oak Knoll Avenue
Napa Valley, CA 94558
Telephone: (707) 255-2200

Four rooms, each with private bath and fireplace. Complimentary full breakfast served at a communal table, tables for two, or in your room. Complimentary early evening wine and hors d'oeuvres. Swimming pool and spa. No disabled access. Smoking is not permitted inside. Guests staying on a Saturday night must stay three nights total. Four-night minimum stay required during holiday periods. Deluxe.

Getting There
Heading north on Highway 29 from Napa, turn right on Oak Knoll Avenue (second right turn after the Salvador Avenue traffic light). Follow Oak Knoll to Big Ranch Road and turn left. Make a quick right back onto Oak Knoll to inn on left.

Oak Knoll Inn

Napa Valley

For those who enjoy the environs of central Napa Valley but who prefer country atmosphere to the faster pace of Napa proper, we heartily recommend Oak Knoll Inn, without question one of the valley's preeminent romantic getaway destinations.

Situated amid vineyards north of town, the three-and-a-half-acre property offers wide valley views and unobstructed vistas of the eastern mountains, along with amenities like a swimming pool and large communal spa. Husband-and-wife innkeepers Barbara Passino and John Kuhlmann have more recently created an organic vegetable, herb, and flower garden which provides home-grown goodies for breakfast and an evening social. They also supply binoculars so guests may enjoy the colorful local bird life.

Rooms for Romance

Operated as an inn since 1984 and redecorated since we first enjoyed a night here, Oak Knoll consists of a nicely updated farmhouse (the parlor area) off of which two stone-walled guest room wings were added, forming an L shape. In terms of size, the rooms at Oak Knoll are among the most generous we've sampled in our travels. Each has plush carpeting, a king-sized brass bed, a woodburning fireplace that can be seen from the bed, and a cozy sitting area with love seat and cushy chairs. All rooms have small outdoor seating areas.

Each hideaway has walls of locally quarried stone and soaring beamed ceilings. Walls between rooms are double-thick, although occasional local traffic can be heard from Oak Knoll Avenue, which runs behind the property. The windowed bathrooms are bright and modern with a tub-and-shower combination in each.

Our personal favorites are Rooms 1 and 6; both are end units and offer the most privacy as well as tall, arched windows with vineyard views. Room rates are in the mid to high $300 range.

In addition to sumptuous accommodations, Oak Knoll treats guests to an outstanding full breakfast as well as an evening wine and cheese reception.

Foothill House

3037 Foothill Boulevard
Calistoga, CA 94515
Telephone: (707) 942-6933 or
toll-free: (800) 942-6933

Three rooms and one cottage, each with private
bath and woodburning fireplace or woodburning
stove, CD player, television, videocassette player,
terry robes, small refrigerator, and eating area.
Complimentary full breakfast served communally or
delivered to your room. Complimentary wine and
cheese served every evening. Complimentary cookies placed in your room in the evening. No disabled
access. Smoking is not permitted. Two-night minimum stay required during weekends. Moderate to
deluxe.

Getting There
Drive north through Napa Valley on Highway 29.
In Calistoga, the road becomes Highway
128/Foothill Boulevard. Inn is one and a half miles
north of Calistoga on left.

Foothill House

Calistoga

It took a visit to Foothill House outside Calistoga to remind us how romantic outdoor spaces and sounds can be when combined with the right amount of indoor intimacy. It's not that the indoor spaces here are lacking; quite the contrary. It's just that the designers of this retreat so artfully incorporated the beauty of nature into the overall scheme.

One of the smallest of our wine country destinations, Foothill House is a country farmhouse that's been updated and converted into a luxury inn with just four rooms. Part of the main house now serves as a gathering place that includes a pretty, glass-enclosed dining area facing the backyard and gazebo.

Rooms for Romance

We've yet to discover a California guest room that rivals—in terms of romantic appeal — the freestanding Quail's Roost. Situated at the top of the property, this striking contemporary cottage has it all: a king-sized four-poster bed, a raised, double-walled woodburning fireplace that can be viewed from bed and bath, a spacious sitting area with a cushy couch and entertainment center, a romantic reading nook with daybed, a kitchen (you may not want to leave for dinner), and woodsy views from the windows.

The glorious bathroom contains not only a spa tub for two but a shower for two. The glass wall in the shower looks out on your private waterfall. French doors open to a private patio. The rate is around $300, but this ultimate honeymoon haven is well worth it.

Our other favorite here is the Evergreen Suite (low $200 range), an impressive, four-hundred-square-foot stunner with a king-sized canopied bed, an inviting alcove for reading and relaxing, a love seat facing a brick fireplace, and a small table and chairs set placed next to a large bay window. Outside is your enclosed private deck with a gently running fountain. The spa tub in the bathroom was designed for one.

A recent addition to the inn is the cozy Redwood Room (high $100 range), accessed by a private entrance at the back of the inn. Outside are a private patio, a redwood tree, and a rock garden. Inside you'll be greeted by a sitting area with a love seat, a fireplace, a queen-sized, four-poster bed, and a bathroom offering both a shower and a spa tub for two.

The Foothill Lupine Suite (mid to upper $100 range) is situated next to the office and faces the parking area. It's a long, deep room furnished with a king-sized bed, a love seat, a small table and chairs set at the center, and a woodburning stove at the far end. The bathroom is equipped with a tub-and-shower combination.

GAIGE HOUSE INN

13540 Arnold Drive
Glen Ellen, CA 95442
Telephone: (707) 935-0237

Thirteen rooms, each with private bath; three rooms with tubs for two. Complimentary full breakfast served at tables for two. Swimming pool and spa. Disabled access. Smoking is not permitted. Two-night minimum stay required during weekends; two-to-three-night minimum stay required during holiday periods. Expensive to deluxe.

Getting There
From Sonoma, follow Highway 12 north and turn left at the sign to Glen Ellen on Arnold Drive. Follow to inn on right prior to reaching Glen Ellen.

Gaige House Inn

Glen Ellen

*I*n Northern California's wine country, bed-and-breakfast inns are about as plentiful as the wines produced here. And just as it takes a tasting critic to help wine lovers choose from among myriad vintages, it takes a traveling critic to help couples sort through the dozens of B&Bs, too many of which play fast and loose with the term "romantic." It's a tough job, but . . .

Our search for Sonoma County's most romantic bed-and-breakfast inn came to an abrupt end when we happened upon Gaige House Inn, located off the beaten track in one of the area's smallest and least visited towns—Glen Ellen. Not your typical B&B, Gaige House is more sophisticated than homespun; more stylish than quaint.

Rooms for Romance

The ultimate romantic accommodations here are two luxurious suites in which standard amenities include large whirlpool tubs, fireplaces, and private decks. Formerly the innkeepers' quarters, the Creekside Suite (mid $300 range) also boasts a two-person shower, a private patio with a knock-out view of Calabazas Creek, and a king-sized bed. The designer sheets are hand-ironed on the bed daily.

The beautiful Gaige Suite (low $300 range) occupies a bright corner on the top floor. Under the twelve-foot ceiling is a canopied king-sized bed, a couch, and cushioned chairs. The large bathroom has a very large spa tub, and the outdoor deck wraps around three sides of the suite.

We were also impressed with the inn's two junior suites (high $200 range). Room 10 is a corner garden-view room with a queen-sized bed, a sunny window seat big enough for two, a spa tub and shower for two, and a corner fireplace. Room 5, the other junior suite, has a comfy chaise longue.

Rooms 4 and 9 (mid $200 range) are called fireplace rooms for obvious reasons. Room 9 is a garden-view room and offers a two-person shower.

Kenwood Inn

10400 Sonoma Highway
Kenwood, CA 95452
Telephone: (707) 833-1293

Twelve rooms, each with private bath, fireplace, and stereo. Complimentary full breakfast served at tables for two in dining room. Complimentary bottle of wine provided on arrival. Swimming pool, spa, and health spa. Disabled access. Smoking is not permitted. Two-night minimum stay required during weekends and holiday periods. Deluxe.

Getting There
From Sonoma, drive north on Highway 12 to inn on left in Kenwood. From Highway 101 in Santa Rosa, drive south on Highway 12 to inn on right in Kenwood.

Kenwood Inn

Kenwood

Northern Californians don't need a plane ticket to sample a night in Tuscany; just a tank of gas, minimal imagination, and a reservation at Kenwood Inn, an Italian-style pensione tucked into Sonoma County's enchanting Valley of the Moon. Located only about forty-five minutes from San Francisco, this combination inn and spa is the perfect destination for Northern California couples seeking an escape from the daily grind but who don't relish spending hours and hours getting there.

This intimate resort compound, which sits discreetly behind a wall just off Highway 12 outside the little burg of Kenwood, pampers with enough romantic amenities to keep the two of you occupied day and night. During our visit, we left only for lunch and dinner. A gourmet breakfast is included.

The public rooms and attractive villas that hold the inn's accommodations will give you the feeling of being in a tiny Italian village; all face a garden area and a swimming pool and spa. A lush wild hillside rises at the back of the inn, and across the highway (some traffic noise can be heard) are over a thousand acres of sloping vineyards visible from many of the rooms.

The inn also includes a full-service day spa that at the time of our visit offered about two dozen different kinds of massages, facials, and body treatments.

Rooms for Romance

The Tuscany Suite (about $400) is the inn's honeymoon hideaway. It's located upstairs in the main building and consists of a bedroom with a queen-sized bed, a large living room with a couch and chairs, and a spacious bathroom with a spa tub for two. The view from the ivy-covered tiled balcony is a wine country dream.

We stayed in Room 2 (low $300 range) in one of the inn's newer villas. The second-floor room, one of four in our cozy villa and typical of most of the inn's luxury accommodations, offers a fireplace that's visible from the bed. French doors open to a small private balcony overlooking the swimming pool. The bathroom has a tub-and-shower combination.

Prices quoted above are in effect from April through October. Tariffs are somewhat lower November through March.

The Gables Bed-and-Breakfast Inn
4257 Petaluma Hill Road
Santa Rosa, CA 95404
Telephone: (707) 585-7777

Eight rooms, each with private bath; three with woodburning stoves or fireplaces. Complimentary full breakfast served at communal table or in your room. Complimentary refreshments served every afternoon. Disabled access. Smoking is not permitted. Two-night minimum stay required during weekends; three-night minimum stay required during some holiday weekends. Moderate to expensive.

Getting There
From Highway 101 in Santa Rosa, exit east at Rohnert Park Expressway to Petaluma Hill Road. Turn north on Petaluma Hill Road to inn on left.

The Gables Bed-and-Breakfast Inn

Santa Rosa

*W*e've toured gingerbread-bedecked Victorians from Ferndale to Pacific Grove, but nothing quite compares with this attractive, unusually styled inn. A rare example of high Victorian gothic revival architecture, The Gables is a town landmark, most noted for its fifteen steep gables—hence the inn's name—and numerous striking keyhole-shaped and shuttered windows. Originally the family home of a successful dairyman, the Gables sits on three-and-a-half acres in the country just outside Santa Rosa.

Rooms for Romance

For couples who like to be away from it all, our top pick here is William and Mary's Cottage (low to mid $200 range), a separate retreat away from the main house near Taylor Creek. It's equipped with a woodburning stove, a kitchenette, a spa tub for two, a television, and a video-cassette player. In the main house are seven rooms and suites, all appointed with antique furniture, brass beds with goose down comforters, and fresh flowers.

The largest room in the house is the Garden View Suite (mid $100 range), furnished with a king-sized poster bed and a twin bed set in a small alcove for reading and relaxing. The Parlor Suite (high $100 range) holds a king-sized bed and an Italian marble fireplace.

A nice redwood deck overlooks an expansive back lawn, and a quaint footbridge crosses Taylor Creek to a meadow.

Applewood Inn and Restaurant

13555 Highway 116
Guerneville, CA 95446
Telephone: (707) 869-9093 or
toll-free: (800) 555-8509

Sixteen rooms and suites, each with private bath. Complimentary full breakfast served at tables for two or four. Restaurant, swimming pool, and spa. Disabled access. Smoking is not permitted. Two-night minimum stay required during weekends; three-night minimum stay required during holiday periods. Expensive to deluxe.

Getting There
From Highway 101 two miles north of Santa Rosa, take River Road/Guerneville exit and drive west fourteen miles to Highway 116. Turn left and cross the Russian River, and drive a half-mile to inn on left.

Applewood Inn and Restaurant

Guerneville

After years of unsuccessful searching, we had almost given up hope of finding a suitably romantic retreat in the Guerneville region. Then we followed up on an effusive review of a meal enjoyed at Applewood Inn and Restaurant and hit the jackpot.

Tucked into a lush hillside among the redwoods, this 1920s mission-style mansion made an easy transition from a home to a combination inn and restaurant. Rooms don't have the retro-fitted look of those in some homes-turned-inns, and the public areas are generous and inviting.

A previous owner created ten guest rooms in anticipation of opening an inn, but funds ran short and the grand old home sat vacant for a time during the mid-1980s. That's when San Franciscans Jim Caron and Darryl Notter happened by while on a wine country vacation in 1985. The two bought the place and furnished the guest rooms with a mix of contemporary and antique furnishings.

Since our first visit, Applewood's reputation has flourished, and so has the inn. A new guest building called the Piccola Casa has been created in the style of the original mansion. Applewood's most romantic suites are found here.

Applewood also boasts a new restaurant, a casually elegant eating place with two river rock fireplaces, lofty beamed ceilings, and windows that look out to the redwoods. It is open for dinner Tuesday through Saturday.

Rooms for Romance

The largest accommodation is the Honeymoon Penthouse (low $300 range), located in the Piccola Casa. This nicely windowed hideaway has a fireplace and a beautiful iron bed named "starry night" by its artist creator. The bathroom has a shower for two.

The Slavianka Suite is a woodsy retreat featuring a private sitting room and Native American artifacts. There's also a stone fireplace, a terra cotta fountain on a private terrace, and a spa tub for two.

Other luxurious Piccola Casa suites, which carry prices starting in the low $200 range, offer bedside fireplaces and either dual-head showers or tubs for two. Nicely appointed and romantic rooms in the original mansion are priced from the mid $100 range.

THE HONOR MANSION

14891 Grove Street
Healdsburg, CA 95448
Telephone: (707) 433-4277 or
toll-free: (800) 554-4667

Nine rooms, each with private bath; three with spa
tubs for two; three with showers for two; four with
gas fireplaces. Complimentary full breakfast served
at communal table or tables for two. Round-the-
clock complimentary coffee drink machine. Swimming pool. Smoking is allowed in a designated area.
Two-night minimum stay required during weekends. Three-night minimum stay required during
holiday periods. Expensive to deluxe.

Getting There
From Highway 101 at Healdsburg, take the Dry
Creek Road exit. Drive east on Dry Creek Road and
turn left on Grove Street.

The Honor Mansion

Healdsburg

$\mathcal{G}$enerally overlooked for years by wine country visitors, Healdsburg has gained consider-
able popularity since we first began exploring the region's romantic potential a decade or
so ago. A return trip during the revision of this volume convinced us that this little community merited inclusion in our selection of Northern California romantic getaway destinations.
We selected The Honor Mansion not only for its romantic charm, but for its convenient location an invigorating stroll from the village's engaging and evolving commercial area.

Visitors will also enjoy the inn's lovely backyard and swimming pool, as well as the side
deck and koi pond under an old magnolia tree.

Rooms for Romance

Set on the edge of town, the Italianate-style mansion and its four acres of well landscaped
grounds are home to nine rooms including a separate cottage which particularly caught our
eye. Located a few steps off the main house and the adjacent koi pond, Squire's Cottage (high
$200 range) contains a king-sized canopied bed and love seat, both of which have a view of a
nice corner stone fireplace. There's also an impressive entertainment center with a stereo, a

videocassette player with a tape library, and a
deck area. In the tiled bathroom is a stall
shower and a long clawfoot soaking tub that
might just accommodate both of you.

Other top choices here are two recently
added ultra-romantic suites (high $200
range). Both offer spa tubs situated on private
patios, fireplaces, and videocassette players
with tape libraries. The Rose Garden Suite
also boasts a two-person shower.

Our favorite room in the main house is the
Rose Room (low $200 range), where a gas
fireplace flickers at the foot of a queen-sized
carved antique bed. There's also a sitting area
and a cozy canvas-curtained outdoor porch
furnished in wicker. The bathroom has a
clawfoot tub-and-shower combination.

The Magnolia Room (high $100 range) is a corner room offering a nice view of the century-
old magnolia tree. The room has a sofa for cuddling, a four-poster bed, and a bathroom with a
stall shower.

For romantics on a budget, we recommend the little Angel Oak Room (mid $100 range),
where couples are greeted by hand-painted cherub murals. There's also a long clawfoot tub
with a hand-held shower attachment in the nicely windowed bathroom. The porch off the
Angel and Dogwood rooms has an antique oak table, a rocking chair, and a couch.

The San Francisco Bay Area

DAYTIME DIVERSIONS

San Francisco, one of the world's most romantic cities, is
home to countless places that stir the heart, including the
Shakespeare Garden and the Conservatory of Flowers, both
in Golden Gate Park. Before a picnic in the park, drop by
Molinari's Deli (373 Columbus Avenue) for Italian sand-
wiches and salads.

A twelve-mile coastal bike trail not open to vehicle traffic
is accessible from Half Moon Bay. There's also a trail from
Kelly Beach Park that follows the cliffs and dunes to
Princeton Harbor. Dunes Beach, also in Half Moon Bay, is a
favorite among beach walkers.

There are also beaches, like Heart's Desire, along Tomales
Bay and the Point Reyes National Seashore in Marin County.
At the venerable Johnson's Oysters (follow signs to Drake's
Beach) you can buy oysters in the shell for a beach barbeque.
If a coastal walk sounds appealing, ask your innkeeper for a
local suggestion. Scores of hiking trails crisscross this region.

TABLES FOR TWO

Pasta Moon (315 Main Street, Half Moon Bay) isn't a quiet,
intimate restaurant, but it serves some of the best food along
this part of the coast. Across the street is San Benito House,
long a Half Moon Bay favorite. Moss Beach Distillery (down
the road from Seal Cove Inn) in Moss Beach offers great
meals, ocean views, and a convivial atmosphere.

The Lark Creek Inn (234 Magnolia Avenue) enjoys a
pleasant country setting in Marin County's Larkspur. One of
the prettiest views of San Francisco is served from the tables
at Guaymas, a Mexican restaurant on Main Street in Tiburon.

For one of San Francisco's best views and best meals, try
McCormick & Kuleto's in Ghirardelli Square (corner of Beach
and Larkin streets). The stylish Aqua (252 California Street) is
a good bet for seafood specialties. Cafe Claude (7 Claude
Lane between Bush and Sutter streets) is one of the city's hidden romantic gems. For drinks we can recommend an ocean-
side table (and oysters, of course) at the Cliff House on Point
Lobos Avenue, and the Carnelian Room bar, atop the Bank of
America building at California and Montgomery streets.

The Inn at Saratoga

20645 Fourth Street
Saratoga, CA 95070
Telephone: (408) 867-5020

Forty-six rooms, each with private bath, videocassette player, and patio or deck; seven rooms with
spa tubs for two. Complimentary continental breakfast served in lobby. Guests have use of a local fitness club. Disabled access. Smoking is allowed. No
minimum stay requirements. Expensive to deluxe.

Getting There
From Interstate 280, follow Route 85 south and take
the DeAnza Boulevard exit. Turn right and follow
for three miles. Turn right at intersection marked
Route 9/Big Basin Way. Proceed one-quarter mile
and turn right on Fourth Street. Inn is a half-block
down the hill on right.

The Inn at Saratoga

Saratoga

*D*espite the frenetic pulse of Silicon Valley, which beats only a few miles away, the village of Saratoga has managed to retain a romantic and charming ambience. You won't find tacky souvenir shops or noisy taverns. Instead, art galleries, boutiques, and upscale restaurants abound.

While most Bay Area motorists breeze in only for a few hours of shopping and maybe a meal or two, a night here can be an enchanting experience, especially if your home base is The Inn at Saratoga.

Nestled beside Wildwood Park and Saratoga Creek, beneath sycamore, maple, and eucalyptus trees, the inn holds forty-six rooms, all with floor-to-ceiling windows that take advantage of the wooded view. The five-story structure doesn't resemble a typical country inn, nor can it accurately be described as a motel or hotel; it's an attractive hybrid.

Rooms for Romance

The least expensive rooms (those starting in the high $100 range) are clean and contemporary but fairly standard from a romantic's perspective. We recommend one of the six deluxe, king-bedded rooms with spa tubs for two (mid $200 range). The deep, gently sloping tubs here are even equipped with plastic pillows for the ultimate in relaxation.

Among the most romantic are the Olivia DeHavilland and Joan Fontaine suites, both of which have bathrooms that feature a television, a heated towel rack, double vanities, and a separate shower.

A night at the inn is an especially romantic complement to one of the many concerts held at the beautiful Paul Masson Winery located nearby.

MILL ROSE INN

615 Mill Street
Half Moon Bay, CA 94019
Telephone: (650) 726-8750 or
toll-free: (800) 900-7673

Six rooms, each with private bath, television, video-cassette player, and cassette deck; five with gas fire-place. Amenities include sandals and kimonos, morning newspaper, and complimentary refreshments. Complimentary full champagne breakfast served at tables for two or in your room. Complimentary wine and refreshments served each afternoon. Spa. No disabled access. Smoking is not permitted. Two-night minimum stay required during weekends and holiday periods. Expensive to deluxe.

Getting There
From Highway 1 in Half Moon Bay, drive east on Highway 92 to Main Street and turn right. Follow Main Street to Mill Street and turn right. Inn is two blocks on right. Half Moon Bay is approximately twenty-six miles south of San Francisco, thirty-nine miles from San Jose, and one-hundred-ten miles from Sacramento.

Mill Rose Inn

Half Moon Bay

*J*n our original Northern California guide, the town of Half Moon Bay was unfortunately not represented. Motivated by our own wanderlust and by requests from traveling romantics for overnight recommendations here, we've scouted out a trio of destinations. Those looking to make magical memories in a luxurious setting won't be disappointed with Mill Rose Inn, which in our opinion offers Half Moon Bay's most romantic lodgings.

A white picket fence and an explosion of color from the inn's gardens greet visitors to this charming property set in a neighborhood of modest homes just a couple of blocks from Main Street.

Guests are received in a quaint, historic cottage that houses the common rooms and two guest rooms. A two-story annex with gables and window boxes was added a few years ago and brought four more tantalizing rooms to the inn.

Rooms for Romance

The Mill Rose is one of the coastal area's most exquisitely decorated inns, and the rooms here boast lush window treatments, fireplaces with hand-painted tiles, and tasteful wallpaper.

Two rooms are located just off the reception area in the cottage. Bordeaux Rose (high $200 range), favored by honeymooners, pampers guests with a queen-sized lace-canopied bed. The bathroom has a marble shower and a spa tub for two that is framed by mirrors and stained glass.

Baroque Rose (low $200 range), the only room without a fireplace or a tub big enough for two, is equipped with a queen-sized, half-canopied brass bed. This is the inn's least expensive room.

The rooms in the original cottage are wonderful, but we were most impressed with the more contemporary hideaways in the annex that offer a bit more privacy.

The most expensive of these (high $200 range) is Renaissance Rose, a bright, two-room suite with a king-sized brass-and-porcelain bed and a tiled fireplace. In the spacious bathroom are a clawfoot tub and shower, both of which should accommodate two.

In the low $200 range is Briar Rose, a second-floor room with a window seat, a queen-sized brass-and-porcelain bed, a fireplace, and a bathroom with a clawfoot tub and a shower for two.

Among the most romantic features of the inn is a large garden gazebo that holds a bubbling spa available to guests by reservation.

SEAL COVE INN

221 Cypress Avenue
Moss Beach, CA 94038
Telephone: (650) 728-7325 or
toll-free (800) 995-9987

Ten rooms, each with private bath, fireplace, telephone, and television with videocassette player; two
with tubs for two. Amenities include a video library,
complimentary soft drinks and wine, evening
refreshments, fresh flowers, and daily newspaper.
Complimentary full breakfast served communally in
dining room or continental breakfast served in your
room. Disabled access. Smoking is not permitted.
Two-night minimum stay required during holiday
periods. Expensive to deluxe.

Getting There
From Freeways 280 or 101, take Highway 92 exit in
San Mateo west toward Half Moon Bay. At
Highway 1 turn north and drive six miles to Moss
Beach. Turn left on Cypress Avenue (at the Moss
Beach Distillery sign) to inn on right. Moss Beach is
approximately twenty miles from San Francisco,
fifty miles from San Jose, and one hundred miles
from Sacramento.

Seal Cove Inn

Moss Beach

*A*fter visiting some fifteen thousand inns around the world, guidebook author Karen Brown decided to see what it was like on the other side of the guest book. So in 1991, she and husband Rick Herbert created, from the ground up, Seal Cove Inn, one of the Bay Area's most romantic retreats.

During her extensive European and domestic travels, Karen has seen the good, the bad, and the ugly, and the couple left nothing to chance when it came time to build their own place. They chose a pretty piece of property near the ocean and designed a striking two-story manor with a steep roof and charming dormers.

Guest rooms are spacious, bathrooms are attractive and contemporary, and each room has a woodburning fireplace and either a balcony or a patio accessed via sliding French doors. Grandfather clocks are an additional nice touch to each room. The Herberts also provide attentive service while respecting the hints of visiting couples who prefer privacy.

Rooms for Romance

Unlike some inns where only the most expensive rooms offer romantic promise, each of Seal Cove Inn's accommodations is fit for a memorable weekend for two.

Provence is one of four downstairs rooms, all of which are in the high $100 range. This retreat has a sofa and a queen-sized bed, as well as an antique rocker.

Our home for a night was Rote Rose (low $200 range) on the second floor, with a high, queen-sized Jenny Lind bed. Two cushy chairs faced each other between the bed and corner fireplace.

Another seductive second-floor room is Cypress (mid $200 range), with waxed pine furnishings and a handmade, king-sized Amish tavern bed. A spa tub for two sits under the dormer window in the bathroom.

The inn's largest room is the Fitzgerald (mid to high $200 range), whose centerpiece is a king-sized canopied bed draped with rich fabric. Nearby a matching sofa rests before the fireplace. Juliette balconies provide a pretty view toward the ocean. In the bathroom is a spa tub for two.

The sea is just a short stroll away, and all guest rooms at Seal Cove Inn have park views with glimpses of the ocean through a distant grove of cypress trees.

THE INN SAN FRANCISCO

943 South Van Ness Avenue
San Francisco, CA 94110
Telephone: (415) 641-0188 or
toll-free: (800) 359-0913

Twenty-one rooms, nineteen with private baths;
four with fireplaces; eight with spa tubs. Amenities
include terry robes, refrigerators, fresh flowers, and
chocolates. Some garage parking stalls available at
extra charge. Complimentary full breakfast buffet
taken at tables for two or to your bedroom. Hot tub.
No disabled access. Smoking is not permitted. Two-
night minimum stay required during weekends and
holidays periods. Moderate to expensive.

Getting There

From the Golden Gate Bridge, exit at Lombard
Street and drive to Van Ness Avenue. Turn right on
Van Ness, follow past Market Street onto South Van
Ness to inn. From the Bay Bridge, follow signs to
Highway 101 north/Golden Gate Bridge. Exit on
Mission Street to the right and drive to South Van
Ness Avenue. Turn right on South Van Ness to inn
between Twentieth and Twenty-First streets.

The Inn San Francisco

San Francisco

One of San Francisco's earliest Victorian mansions, this grand Italianate occupies a spot in an ethnically diverse, blue-collar neighborhood in the Mission District on what was long ago known as Mansion Row, an authentic collection of grand homes that barely escaped the fires following the 1906 earthquake.

In contrast to the neighborhood bustle, the inn is quiet and peaceful inside. Steep stairs lead from the street to the entry and to ornate double parlors. More stairs lead to the second and third floors, and a narrow, almost vertical staircase spirals to a breezy rooftop sundeck that overlooks the city.

Rooms for Romance

Rooms classified as "cozy" are priced in the low $100 range. Some of these share bathrooms and have double beds. We don't recommend these for romantic getaways. Those in the "spacious" category have queen-sized feather beds and private baths, and carry rates in the upper $100 range. Deluxe rooms, like those described below, have tariffs in the low to mid $200 range, and are equipped with spas, hot tubs, and/or fireplaces.

As is often the case in older San Francisco homes, many rooms whose windows are shaded by adjacent buildings are somewhat dark and tend to feature creative uses of space. In some rooms, it appears that bathrooms were once closets and closets used to be crawl spaces. It's fun to sit back and imagine the history behind the sturdy manse.

Room 24 is a second-floor hideaway that overlooks the inn's garden. The room is decorated with darkly stained woods and deep-colored rugs, and holds a queen-sized feather bed. A velveteen couch is set beside a fireplace screen (no fireplace, however). The bathtub area, separated from the actual bathroom, is awash in sunlight and features a deep whirlpool tub for two.

Room 21 (upper $100 range) is a vision in red, with rich Oriental rugs and a fluffy queen-sized feather bed dressed in a crimson spread. An antique chaise longue sits by a lace-curtained bay window overlooking South Van Ness Avenue. The room also has a decorative fireplace, complete with statues and carved tile, and a shower with a tiny, custom-made square bathtub.

The Garden Cottage Suite (low $200 range) has a queen-sized bed and two twin-sized beds, a separate sitting room, a fireplace, a private bath, and a deep spa tub for two.

A garden gazebo holds a communal hot tub that's available twenty-four hours a day. Terry robes are provided in each room.

Mandarin Oriental

222 Sansome Street
San Francisco, CA 94104
Telephone: (415) 276-9888 or
toll-free: (800) 622-0404

One hundred fifty-eight rooms, each with private bath and tub for two. Amenities include refrigerators, daily newspaper, robes, and silk slippers. Restaurant and lounge on ground level. Disabled access. Smoking is allowed. No minimum night stay required. Deluxe.

Getting There

From the Bay Bridge, exit at Fremont Street and continue across Market Street to Front Street (Fremont Street becomes Front Street). Turn left on Pine Street and right on Sansome Street. From the San Francisco Airport, follow Highway 101 north and exit at Fourth and Bryan streets. Turn left on Third Street, cross Market Street (which becomes Kearny Street), and drive three blocks to Bush Street. Turn right on Bush Street and left on Sansome Street.

Mandarin Oriental

San Francisco

*T*he Mandarin Oriental is proof that romance doesn't necessarily go exclusively hand-in-hand with small cozy country inns. Our largest recommended Northern California destination, this lavish one-hundred-fifty-eight-room hotel offers what must rank as one of the most romantic experiences in all the world.

The hotel occupies the top eleven floors of the forty-eight-story twin California Center towers, connected by glass-enclosed skybridges on the guest room floors. Guests here are treated to dizzying views of San Francisco along with luxury appointments.

Rooms for Romance

All rooms boast breathtaking city views, and each is furnished with three telephones, a sitting area, and a marble bathroom with deep soaking tub for two. Rates start in the high $300 range for what is described as a Deluxe room with a king-sized bed.

The premier romantic retreats are the twenty-two Mandarin Rooms, where spacious windowed bathrooms feature panoramic city and bay views from the tub. As you might expect, such bliss carries a price—about $500 a night (binoculars provided). However, this is an experience you'll not soon forget.

Downtown hotels in San Francisco cater to business travelers and consequently charge more during the work week. If you're planning a weekend stay, be sure to ask about the availability of special lower rates. You may be pleasantly surprised at the savings.

Hotel Sausalito

16 El Portal
Sausalito, CA 94965
Telephone: (415) 332-0700 or
toll-free: (888) 442-0700

Sixteen rooms and suites, each with private bath, telephone, and television. Complimentary morning coffee and pastries served at adjacent cafe. Disabled access. Smoking is not permitted. Two-night minimum stay required during weekends. Expensive to deluxe.

Getting There
From Highway 101 north of the Golden Gate Bridge, take the Sausalito exit and follow for approximately two miles into the village. The hotel is at the corner of Bridgeway and El Portal across from Vina del Mar Park.

Hotel Sausalito

Sausalito

In its early days, the Sausalito Hotel had a wild reputation. Built in 1915, the hostelry was reputed to have served both as a bordello and as a refuge for bootleggers during Prohibition. Over the past several years of visiting this romantic waterside village, we've watched the hotel pass through various incarnations, first as a hippy hangout, then as a modestly upgraded hotel for weekend wanderers. But it was the most recent renovation that really caught our eye. Completely redone in the mid-1990s, the stylish Sausalito Hotel of today is a beacon for romantic travelers.

A cadre of designers and artisans was engaged to transform the aging hotel into an upscale, Mediterranean, boutique-style inn. The apricot, yellow, and terra cotta tones are warm and restful, and faux finishes are employed liberally throughout the establishment. Nearly everything in the inn is handmade.

Rooms for Romance

For a romantic getaway, we limit our recommendations to the hotel's two suites and Park View rooms.

The Sausalito Suite (high $200 range) is a spacious, lushly draped, and nicely windowed suite that overlooks the quaint village shops along Bridgeway. The suite has a sitting area with a couch and a table, and the tiled bathroom holds a large shower and a small sink.

The hotel's rounded corner Park Suite (mid $200 range) overlooks village shops and the little park across the street (see photo on previous page) and offers a peek of the bay. There's a king-sized bed and a romantic turreted sitting area with a table and two chairs.

Among the smallish Park View rooms (high $100 range) is Room 209, furnished with a queen-sized bed and offering a large bay window overlooking the park and fountain, the bay, and the hills of Belvedere. Two small chairs provide the only seating for the two of you. The petite bathroom holds a pedestal sink and a tub-and-shower combination.

Those intent on keeping in touch with the outside world will appreciate the desktop phones with computer data ports, voice mail, and in-room fax machines available on request. The morning newspaper is delivered to your door.

Pelican Inn

10 Pacific Way
Muir Beach, CA 94965
Telephone: (415) 383-6000

Seven rooms, each with private bath.
Complimentary full English breakfast served at
tables for two in the restaurant or in your room.
Restaurant and lounge. No disabled access in guest
rooms. Smoking is allowed in guest rooms; no
smoking in dining areas. No minimum night stay
required. Moderate to expensive.

Getting there
From Highway 101 north of Sausalito, take the
Highway 1/Stinson Beach exit. At the junction (gas
station) turn left toward Stinson Beach. Turn left at
Muir Woods sign and continue on Highway 1 for
two and a half miles to inn.

Pelican Inn

Muir Beach

A romantic slice of sixteenth-century England, Pelican Inn is a Tudor-style farmhouse that's true to its heritage. Low doorjambs, leaded glass windows, English antiques, exposed wooden beams, and full- and half-canopied beds are found throughout the inn. Guest rooms occupy the second floor; a cozy restaurant and pub are located on the ground floor.

The charming half-timbered building enjoys a wooded setting between the ocean and redwoods and is well positioned for a weekend of poking around Marin County's romantic coastal areas. Stinson and Muir beaches are nearby.

There's a restaurant on site with an English-inspired menu and an English-style bar with international selections of beer and wine and the requisite dartboard. A hearty complimentary English breakfast is served in the morning.

Rooms for Romance

Rooms 1 and 7 (low $200 range) are the largest in the inn. These hold couches while the others have chairs. Room 7 sits under the eaves and has a dormer window.

Little Room 2 (high $100 range), oft requested and referred to as the "cute room," features a bed that's tucked beneath a cozy, timbered canopy frame.

Rooms 3, 4, and 5 (around $200) have balconies and overlook the parking area and the

woods. Rooms 1, 2, 6, and 7 overlook the lawn, hills, and fields with horses. All rooms have queen-sized beds.

Bathrooms, while not lavish in space or amenities, are functional, just like those of Olde England. All have tiled showers except Room 7, which has a bathtub.

MOUNTAIN HOME INN

810 Panoramic Highway
Mill Valley, CA 94941
Telephone: (415) 381-9000

Ten rooms, each with private bath; five with fire-places. Complimentary full breakfast served at tables for two or in your room. Restaurant and lounge. Disabled access. Smoking is allowed in half of the rooms. No minimum night stay required. Moderate to expensive.

Getting There
From the Golden Gate Bridge, exit Highway 101 at Stinson Beach/Highway 1 in Mill Valley. Drive about two-thirds of a mile and turn left at the stoplight onto Highway 1. Follow for two and a half miles. At the Panoramic Highway (the sign says Mt. Tamalpais), turn right and drive for nearly one mile. At the four-way intersection, take the high road, Panoramic. Drive for two miles to inn on right.

Mountain Home Inn

Mill Valley

*T*he often puzzled responses elicited by our mention of the Mountain Home Inn confirm that there are still a few secret places left in the San Francisco Bay Area.

Only about a half-hour's drive from downtown San Francisco, this Marin County hideaway has a lush setting on the lower reaches of 2,600-foot-high Mount Tamalpais. The terraced guest room buildings afford gorgeous views of San Francisco Bay, the Tiburon Peninsula, and Mount Diablo. San Francisco's beloved newspaper columnist Herb Caen described the inn as a miniature version of Yosemite's grand Ahwahnee Hotel.

Rooms for Romance

Rooms 1 and 5, called deluxe rooms (mid $200 range), are the most romantic and the most expensive. Both have fireplaces and king-sized beds. Room 1 has a skylight. The bathrooms in these rooms, equipped with spa tubs, open through shutters to the bedrooms and the beautiful views beyond.

Room 6, a similarly equipped retreat located on a lower level facing the redwoods, is available for about $10 less. Room 10, which has a bay window and spa tub for two but no fireplace, commands a rate of around $200.

"Fireplace guest rooms" with terraces are available in the high $100 range. Standard rooms, furnished with queen-sized bed, are offered in the mid $100 range. Some have private terraces.

If there's no room at the inn during your visit to Marin County, you can always drop by for a romantic lunch or appetizers on the deck overlooking the north Bay Area or at a dining room table next to a fireplace. And don't overlook the romantic vistas from atop Mount Tam just a short drive from the inn.

Gerstle Park Inn

34 Grove Street
San Rafael, CA 94901
Telephone: (415) 721-7611 or
toll-free: (800) 726-7611

Ten suites and two cottages, each with private bath.
Complimentary full breakfast served at small tables
or on the verandas. Complimentary wine served
each evening. Disabled access. Smoking is not permitted. Two-night minimum stay required during
weekends. Expensive to deluxe.

Getting There
From Highway 101 north of San Anselmo, take the
Central San Rafael exit and drive west on Third
Street. Turn left on D Street and right on San Rafael
Avenue. Turn left on Grove Street; inn is on the
right.

Gerstle Park Inn

San Rafael

*D*on't let the fact that this rural property recently celebrated its one hundredth birthday lead you to believe you'll be sleeping in drafty quarters, trudging down the hall to the bathroom, or treading on squeaky floors. Gerstle Park Inn is all about contemporary romantic comforts all wrapped up in a striking estate that's a must-stop on San Rafael's walking tour of historic homes.

The inn occupies one-and-a-half acres and consists of the large main building—formerly part of the old Lewis Sloss estate—and an adjacent carriage house, which now holds two large suites with kitchens. The secluded property, lush with mature trees, hillside pasture, and fruit orchard, is a short walk to downtown San Rafael, with its great shops and restaurants.

Rooms for Romance

Guests staying in the remote Lodge Suite (around $200) have a private Dutch door entrance and their own deck. Inside the suite, decorated in French style with blue and soft yellow color schemes, are a separate parlor with cushy furnishings and a bedroom with a king-sized bed. There's also a spa tub for two.

Another recommended romantic choice is the Redwood Suite (high $100 range), a second-floor hideaway reached by a private stairway. The nicely windowed corner room has a sitting area with a couch, a king-sized bed, and a spa tub for one. French doors lead to a deck with a garden view. The two-room Oak Suite (high $100 range) has similar amenities.

On the main floor is the Leonhard Suite (high $100 range), which features an eighteenth-century French bedroom set. The bed is king-sized, and the suite also has a spa tub. The Gerstle Suite (upper $100 range) has a steam bath. We should point out that the Leonhard suite overlooks the inn's parking area.

The spacious Sunset and Sunrise Suites (upper $100 range) are located on the top level of the adjacent carriage house and feature kitchens, living rooms with dining areas, and separate bedrooms. Both have private outdoor areas. The Sunset Suite has a double bed; the bed in the Sunrise Suite is queen-sized.

Ten Inverness Way Bed and Breakfast

10 Inverness Way
Inverness, CA 94937
Telephone: (415) 669-1648

Five rooms, each with private bath. Complimentary
full breakfast served at communal tables. Spa. No
disabled access. Smoking is not permitted. Two-
night minimum stay required during weekends;
three-night minimum during holiday periods.
Moderate.

Getting There
From Highway 101 north of San Francisco, take the
San Anselmo/Sir Francis Drake Boulevard exit, and
follow Sir Francis Drake for about a half-hour to
Highway 1. Make a right turn on Highway 1 and an
immediate left on Bear Valley Road. Drive about
three miles to stop sign and turn left, following road
for four miles to Inverness. Turn left at the second
Inverness Way sign. Inn is on the right.

Ten Inverness Way Bed and Breakfast

Inverness

A warning to traveling romantics: like kryptonite sapped the strength of Superman, a night at Ten Inverness Way will rob you of tension. Why, just the sight of this charming, shingled inn, surrounded by flowers, plants, and trees, drove the stress from our road-weary bodies and made us want to simply melt away into a couch. A walk up the stairs to the homey second-level living area made us want to slink into a couch and melt away.

Since our first visit the inn has changed ownership, and the exterior and interior have been freshened up. The furnishings in the common area have been redone, and guest rooms have received new linens and featherbeds.

Rooms for Romance

Situated on the lower level near the entry, Room 3 (high $100 range) is the inn's most spacious and most private. Inside are a love seat, a small table and chairs, and a tiny kitchen. The bathroom has a tub and shower combination. French doors open onto a private gravel garden patio.

Room 4 is a nicely lit corner that faces the rear and side of the property. Room 5 offers a view of trees from the bed. Tomales Bay is partially visible from Room 2, a front-facing room whose bathroom is placed under a skylit eave. These rooms, whose bathrooms are equipped with showers, are offered in the mid $100 range.

Because the rooms here are quite small (most are furnished with but one cushy chair in addition to a queen-sized bed), guests tend to congregate in the inn's comfortable living room, which contains a stone fireplace, sofas, and chairs, in addition to a guitar. Couples may also reserve time in the very private hot tub room at the rear of the property, accessed by a garden path.

The Monterey Bay Area

DAYTIME DIVERSIONS

Tor House, the enchanting stone farmhouse of poet
Robinson Jeffers, is open for tours Fridays and Saturdays.
You'll find it at 26304 Ocean View Avenue near Stewart
Way in Carmel. Just inside the lower gate of Carmel
Mission, follow Mission Trail to a meadow with a couple
of benches. Be sure to take time out from shopping for a
stroll along the white sandy beach in Carmel.

At the foot of Forest Avenue in Pacific Grove is popular Lovers Point Park, which offers a sandy cove and beautiful vistas. A spectacular bay-side bike/walking path con-
nects Pacific Grove with Monterey via Cannery Row.

Santa Cruz visitors will enjoy a bicycle ride on an
equally impressive pedestrian/bike trail that winds along
West Cliff Drive between the wharf and Natural Bridges
State Park. The city's downtown Pacific Garden Mall has
rebounded from the 1989 earthquake.

TABLES FOR TWO

In Carmel, our innkeepers pointed us to the Flying Fish
Grill (between Ocean and Seventh) and gave the most
stars to Sans Souci (Lincoln Avenue between Fourth and
Fifth avenues) and to Anton and Michel (Mission Street
at Seventh Avenue).

Critics have singled out Monterey's Stokes Adobe
restaurant (500 Hartnell Street) as among the best on the
Monterey Peninsula.

In Pacific Grove, The Centrella (see listing in this section) is within walking distance of the Old Bath House
(620 Ocean View Boulevard), a restaurant that overlooks
the bay.

The Shadowbrook restaurant in Capitola (1750 Wharf
Road) is one of Northern California's most romantic dining spots. A funicular transports diners down a steep
wooded hillside to the restaurant nestled beside the quiet
Soquel River.

BABBLING BROOK INN

1025 Laurel Street
Santa Cruz, CA 95060
Telephone: (831) 427-2437 or
toll-free: (800) 866-1131

Thirteen rooms, each with private bath, television, and fireplace. Complimentary full breakfast buffet taken at tables for two in the lobby area or taken to your room. Complimentary wine and cheese served each afternoon. Disabled access. Smoking is allowed only on outside decks. Two-night minimum stay required for Saturday reservations. One-night Saturday stay available at extra cost. Moderate to expensive.

Getting There
From Highway 17 or Highway 1 in Santa Cruz, follow signs to Highway 1 north/Half Moon Bay. (Highway 1 is called Mission Street in Santa Cruz.) Follow Mission Street to Laurel Street and turn left. Follow Laurel Street to inn on right.

Babbling Brook Inn

Santa Cruz

*M*any inns—some with dramatic ocean views—have opened in the Santa Cruz area in recent years. To many central coast visitors, however, the Babbling Brook Inn, Santa Cruz's first B & B, remains the favorite, despite its location several blocks away from the ocean.

Occupying a lush setting along the banks of a creek from which it draws its name, the Babbling Brook consists of a historic residence that houses five rooms and three attractive, two-story brown-shingled buildings that hold the other eight rooms. Each has a view of the brook or the romantic gardens. There's even a quaint little covered bridge and a waterwheel.

Visitors should be aware that the Babbling Brook Inn is situated along a somewhat busy residential street, and traffic can be heard from some rooms, especially during the daytime. The beach and the Santa Cruz Municipal Wharf are within walking distance. A bike trail runs for several miles along enchanting West Cliff Drive from the wharf to Natural Bridges State Park.

Rooms for Romance

Operated by the folks who own Capitola's Inn at Depot Hill (next listing), the Babbling Brook tempts visitors with a delectable variety of country French-styled accommodations. This isn't your typical, four- or five-room B & B. It'll take you thirteen visits to sample all the rooms here.

The Pissaro (mid $100 range) features a hexagonal window area that looks over the brook and a private garden-level deck accessed through French doors. There's also a deep soaking tub that, alas, is only big enough for one.

The Fern Grotto Room (mid $100 range) conveys a decidedly English feel. This room contains a queen-sized bed with flowing drapes, a large sitting area, and a corner radiant heat fireplace. A private balcony overlooks the inn's huge waterwheel. In the bathroom is an antique clawfoot bathtub.

The centerpiece of the Degas Room (mid $100 range) is an impressive ten-foot-tall, white wrought-iron bed created for a production of *Romeo and Juliet* at the University of California, Santa Cruz. This cozy room sits right above the brook.

In the FMRS Garden Room (mid $100 range), a large window overlooks the garden. This room is equipped with a radiant heat fireplace and a king-sized bed, and the bathroom here is the inn's largest.

Monet (high $100 range), a second-floor room overlooking the garden and brook, has a bathroom with a spa tub for two set under a pentagonal window and a skylight. The room has a queen-sized bed, a corner woodstove, and a balcony overlooking the inn's waterfall and footbridge.

THE INN AT DEPOT HILL

250 Monterey Avenue
Capitola, CA 95010
Telephone: (831) 462-3376 or
toll-free: (800) 572-2632

Twelve rooms, each with private bath, private entry, gas or woodburning fireplace, tub or shower for two, robes, television with videocassette player, and cassette stereo system. Complimentary full breakfast served at communal table, tables for two, or in your room. Disabled access. Smoking is permitted on private patios only. Two-night minimum required if staying on a Saturday night or during holiday periods. Expensive to deluxe.

Getting There
From Highway 1 south of Santa Cruz, take the Park Avenue exit west toward the bay. After one mile, turn left on Monterey Avenue and make an immediate left into the inn's parking lot.

The Inn at Depot Hill

Capitola

Thank your lucky stars for the demise of the train that once shuttled San Francisco passengers to the beach community of Capitola. Had the old "Suntan Special" not given way to the automobile, The Inn at Depot Hill might still be a cold and drab railway station.

The 1901-vintage depot had been serving as a private residence when owner Suzie Lankes and partner Dan Floyd arrived on the scene a few years ago. Ten months of new construction and renovation created what is now one of the central coast's most luxurious inns.

Although Lankes first considered modeling the guest rooms after the luxurious Orient Express, she ultimately headed in a different direction, instilling them with the essence of various destinations that might once have been served by vintage trains. These days your ticket will take you to such storied locales as Portofino and Paris.

Rooms for Romance

Since our first visit, four new rooms have been added. The Orient Express Suite (mid $200 range) is a three-tiered hideaway where a queen-sized featherbed, a gas fireplace, and a television occupy the lower level. The second level is a reading area, while the third level is a loft that resembles a Pullman sleeping railcar with a faux window looking out on the countryside of Europe. The bathroom has a shower for two.

The three other new additions are located in an adjacent building. Here a black slate stairway with Japanese-style lighting leads to an oriental garden, the setting for the Kyoto Room (high $200 range). Shoji screens slide across glass doors that look out onto a private garden. You will love the Japanese soaking tub for two with a dragon faucet and the shower that simulates rainfall.

Costa del Sol (low $200 range) is decorated in blues and yellows, and has a hand-painted Mediterranean tiled gas fireplace, a king-sized, half-canopied bed, and a tiled deck. Valencia (high $200 range) has a large sitting area with a fireplace, a dining area with a round stone table, and a bathroom with a soaking tub for two.

The Paris Room (low $200 range), which opens onto the inn's main garden, is specially designed for a lusty getaway. A fireplace separates the living room and bedroom, whose windows are covered with French lace. Soft lighting from Louis XVI lamps completes the mood. In the black-and-white marbled bathroom is a spacious shower with a spigot for each of you.

Those for whom a visit to a former depot wouldn't be complete without a night aboard a train will not be disappointed with the sumptuous Railroad Baron's Room (mid $200 range), bedecked with rich trappings like those enjoyed in the private Pullman cars of yesteryear. Warm dark woods, gold leafing, upholstered walls, and tassled draperies are combined with a sumptuous bathroom with a deep tub for two. Even if you don't sleep in this spectacular room, ask to see it if it's vacant. All aboard!

Hotel Pacific

300 Pacific Street
Monterey, CA 93940
Telephone: (831) 373-5700 or
toll-free: (800) 554-5542

One hundred five rooms, each with private bath, fireplace, two televisions, and three telephones. Amenities include terry robes, refrigerators, underground parking, room service, and concierge service. Complimentary continental breakfast served communally; can be delivered to your room for a small charge. Courtyard spas. Disabled access. Smoking is allowed. Two-night minimum stay required during weekends and holiday periods. Expensive to deluxe.

Getting There
From Highway 1, take the Soledad exit in Monterey and proceed through the stop light. Turn right on Pacific Street and follow to inn downtown.

Hotel Pacific

Monterey

*A*mong the newest of our recommended coastal destinations, Hotel Pacific is a great place to stay for those who delight in the sights, smells, and sounds of the coast and who enjoy the contemporary conveniences—like underground parking and room service—that a newer hotel has to offer.

In Monterey's historically rich downtown, peppered with graceful Spanish-style buildings, Hotel Pacific blends nicely with a colorfully landscaped adobe-style facade. Cars are tucked conveniently out of sight in a parking garage below the guest rooms. It appears much smaller than its one-hundred-five-room size would indicate.

The hotel is a collection of more than a dozen tiered structures built around three courtyards. They're connected by a maze of pathways made of terra cotta tiles, and the grounds are lush with plants and flowers. Hotel Pacific is not billed as an ocean-view hotel, although a few rooms do offer a peek.

Rooms for Romance

Wood, plaster, and tile figure prominently in the guest rooms. The goose down feather beds are posted with peeled logs, and hardwood floors are covered with handwoven rugs. All rooms have fireplaces and private patios or balconies and are equipped with two televisions (one is in the bathroom) and three telephones. Tubs and separate showers are found in each bathroom.

Suite 426 (high $300 range), our home for a night, was an end unit in which the draped king-

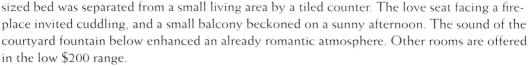

sized bed was separated from a small living area by a tiled counter. The love seat facing a fireplace invited cuddling, and a small balcony beckoned on a sunny afternoon. The sound of the courtyard fountain below enhanced an already romantic atmosphere. Other rooms are offered in the low $200 range.

Hotel Pacific is within walking distance of Fisherman's Wharf, historic sites, and the Monterey-to-Pacific Grove pedestrian/bicycle path that runs through Cannery Row. Also a short stroll away are the peninsula's longest stretch of beach and the popular Monterey Bay Aquarium.

At the time of our visit, the hotel was offering various specially priced getaway packages available Sunday through Thursday.

THE CENTRELLA

612 Central Avenue
Pacific Grove, CA 93950
Telephone: (831) 372-3372 or
toll free: (800) 233-3372

Twenty-six rooms, all with private bath; five rooms
with fireplaces. Complimentary full breakfast buffet;
seating at communal tables and tables for two.
Complimentary wine and appetizers served every
afternoon. Disabled access. Smoking is not permitted. Two-night minimum stay on weekends.
Moderate to deluxe.

Getting There
From southbound Highway 1, take Pebble
Beach/Pacific Grove exit (Highway 68 west) and
follow signs to Pacific Grove. Continue on Forest
Avenue into downtown Pacific Grove, cross
Lighthouse Avenue, and drive one block to Central
Avenue. Turn left on Central Avenue and drive two
blocks to inn.

The Centrella

Pacific Grove

*I*t seems like yesterday that we watched workers transform an ugly duckling into a graceful swan. When we first happened by the decrepit, hundred-year-old boarding house in the early 1980s, it appeared as though the building was being torn down. Actually, the owners left the weathered but elegant facade intact and completely gutted the interior. In the process they created The Centrella, an upscale inn with a handsome vintage appearance.

Occupying a sunny corner in a residential area, the green, cream, and maroon-trimmed inn is a short walk from the bay as well as from quaint downtown shops and restaurants.

Breakfast and late afternoon refreshments are laid out in a spacious parlor/dining room. Guests may sit at tables of six or eight or at small tables for two against windows that face a side garden area.

Rooms for Romance

There are seven rooms on the first floor, but for romantic reasons we prefer the top two floors of the main building and the five adjacent cottage units. The top floor is given to two spacious suites with dormer windows, each offered in the $200 range. In the Vera Franklin Suite, a pretty, queen-sized brass-and-iron bed is illuminated by two skylights. A sitting area with a settee and cushy chair is situated under the eaves. The dormer window offers a peek of Monterey Bay.

The adjacent Anna Bieghle Suite has skylights, a king-sized bed, and a sitting area with a love seat and wet bar. The bathrooms of both suites have pedestal sinks and clawfoot tubs.

Our favorite on the second floor is Room 22 (low to mid $100 range), a nicely windowed corner with matching floral-print wallpaper and draperies. The king-sized brass and iron bed, dressed in pretty white linens, is flanked by antique tables with small stained-glass lamps. There's a clawfoot tub in the bathroom.

Just off the inn's rose garden sits the storybook-style R. L. Holman Suite ($200 range), decorated in coral and heather-green tones. This spacious retreat has a bay window with a table and two chairs and a living room with a wet bar, a television, and a sofa facing a fireplace. In the bedroom is a queen-sized iron bed.

The John Steinbeck Suite (upper $200 range) is a second-story cottage unit that includes a living room with a fireplace and a sofa and a separate bedroom with a king-sized bed.

Furnishings at The Centrella are a comfortable mix of antique beds and dressers, chairs, sofas with contemporary fabrics, and wicker.

GATEHOUSE INN BED AND BREAKFAST

225 Central Avenue
Pacific Grove, CA 93950
Telephone: (831) 649-8436 or
toll-free: (800) 753-1881

Nine rooms, each with private bath; four with wood stoves. Complimentary full buffet breakfast served at communal table and tables for two, or taken to your room. Complimentary refreshments available round-the-clock. Smoking is not permitted. Two-night minimum stay required during weekends. Moderate to expensive.

Getting There
From southbound Highway 1, take Pebble Beach/Pacific Grove exit (Highway 68 west) and follow signs to Pacific Grove. Continue on Forest Avenue and turn right at Central Avenue. Drive seventeen blocks to inn.

Gatehouse Inn Bed and Breakfast

Pacific Grove

*A*lthough we've been combing the streets of this Victorian village for years, we continue to uncover new romantic secrets like this charmer situated only about a block from the bay.

Reportedly admired by novelist John Steinbeck, whose family lived across the street, the Gatehouse was built in 1884 by a California senator as a summer home. In more recent years the interior has been tastefully redone to provide niceties, such as private baths and fireplaces, that traveling couples appreciate.

Unlike some dark and dreary Victorians we've visited, the Gatehouse is a particularly bright, airy, and cheerful structure, especially on those sunny days that paint the Monterey Bay skies a vivid blue. Several rooms have bay views.

Rooms for Romance

The Captain's Room, our personal favorite, is accessed via a separate entrance around the back of the house. This remote hideaway has a private covered porch and looks out over a small side yard to the bay. The private bathroom, whose door has a ship's porthole, has a clawfoot tub.

The bay-view Langford Room (upper $100 range) is probably the inn's most romantically styled room and the one that offers the best view to the water. Enlarged from two smaller rooms, this sunny corner holds a raised queen-sized bed. Next to the bed is a pretty, white antique wood stove that shares a tiled hearth with a clawfoot tub. The original wood floors are covered with area rugs.

At the rear of the house on the second floor is the Wicker Room (mid $100 range), a smaller room with a queen-sized white iron bed. The windowed walls afford a sweeping view of Monterey Bay, and the bathroom contains a clawfoot tub.

Also worthy of note is the second-floor Turkish Room (low $100 range), where an artfully papered ceiling design will entertain you from the queen-sized brass bed. The Turkish and Cannery Row rooms are the inn's two most unusually decorated accommodations. We weren't particularly impressed with the Italian Room as a romantic retreat.

La Playa Hotel

Camino Real at Eighth Avenue (P.O. Box 900)
Carmel, CA 93921
Telephone: (831) 624-6476 or
toll-free: (800) 582-8900

Seventy-five rooms and five cottages, each with
private bath. Swimming pool. Restaurant and
lounge. Disabled access. Smoking is allowed in
certain rooms; non-smoking rooms available. Two-
night minimum stay required during weekends;
three-night minimum stay required during holiday
periods. Moderate to deluxe.

Getting There
From Highway 1, exit at Ocean Avenue and drive
west into Carmel. Turn left on Camino Real to
Eighth Avenue to hotel.

La Playa Hotel Cottages

Carmel

*W*e've long been impressed with the entire La Playa estate, but from a purely romantic perspective, the five dreamy cottages are our favorites. The five cottages, which range in size from one to three bedrooms, are nestled among the pine and cypress trees along a peaceful residential street a block and a half from the main hotel.

Rooms for Romance

The least expensive (low $200 range) is Skyway, a cozy cottage with separate living and sleeping areas, as well as an outdoor terrace.

Two larger cottages, Homeport and Moongate (mid $300 range), are similarly laid out. These have king-sized beds in the bedrooms, fireplaces, full kitchens, and outdoor patios.

The other two cottages, Tradewinds and Loghaven, are intended to house multiple couples and families. These accommodate six and eight people, respectively.

While we've focused our attention on the cottages, La Playa's two hotel buildings hold seventy-five very comfy rooms, some of which offer ocean views.

CARRIAGE HOUSE INN

Junipero Street between Seventh and Eighth
avenues (P.O. Box 1900)
Carmel, CA 93921
Telephone: (408) 625-2585

Thirteen rooms, each with private bath and fireplace; two with tubs for two. Complimentary continental breakfast brought to your room. No disabled
access. Smoking is not permitted. Two-night minimum stay required during weekends and holiday
periods. Expensive to deluxe.

Getting There
From Highway 1, exit at Ocean Avenue and drive
west into Carmel. Turn left on Junipero Street and
drive one and a half blocks to inn on right.

Carriage House Inn

Carmel

We discovered Carriage House Inn during a visit to its charming next-door neighbor, the Cobblestone Inn, which is featured in our first Northern California romantic getaway guide. Fairly nondescript from the outside, Carriage House can only be completely appreciated from the inside, that is if you're lucky enough to book a room. The inn was full during our first visit, and we had to come back another day in order to preview some guest rooms.

Among the inn's special amenities is a continental breakfast selected from a menu and delivered to your room. After-dinner coffee drinks and sherry are also available.

Rooms for Romance

We recommend the upstairs rooms, which have vaulted ceilings and either soaking tubs or spa

tubs designed for one person. Room 3 is an oversized specialty room with a lavish bathroom containing a two-person spa tub. The most often-requested rooms are 12, with a spa tub for one, and 8, with a soaking tub.

The ultimate romantic retreat here is the Master Suite, with separate sitting and bedroom areas along with a woodburning fireplace in each. The sitting room has a sofa bed and the bedroom contains a raised, queen-sized, four-poster bed that requires a step stool to reach. The other rooms have king-sized beds.

At the time of our visit, all but one of the rooms were being offered in the mid $200 range. The Master Suite carries a rate in the low $300 range.

All rooms at Carriage House Inn have fireplaces, antiques, an English country decor, and down pillows and comforters. All rooms except three have cozy window seats by the fire-

places. There are no ocean views; rooms look out onto the trees.

Tickle Pink Inn

155 Highland Drive
Carmel, CA 93923
Telephone: (831) 624-1244 or
toll free: (800) 635-4774

Thirty-five rooms, each with private bath; sixteen with woodburning fireplaces. Amenities include terry robes, daily newspaper, and televisions with videocassette players in all rooms. Complimentary continental breakfast served at tables for two or in your room. Complimentary wine and appetizers served every evening. Lounge. No disabled access. Smoking is allowed. Two-night minimum stay required on weekends; three-night minimum during holiday periods. Expensive to deluxe.

Getting There
From Carmel, drive south on Highway 1 for four miles. Turn left on Highland Drive and follow to inn on right.

Tickle Pink Inn

Carmel

Several decades ago, on the site now occupied by this popular romantic destination, Bess and Edward Tickle lived in a stone cottage overlooking the rugged coast. Inspired by the constant display of flowers—primarily pink ones—in the Tickles' garden, someone suggested they name their little hideaway Tickle Pink.

The original Tickle Pink is long gone, but when the Gurries family built this resort hotel on the Tickle property in the early 1950s, they retained the playful name, which, like that of its neighbor, the Highlands Inn, has since become synonymous with coastal romance in Northern California.

The venerable cliff-side inn is now hosting its second generation of traveling romantics, as evidenced by an inscription found in a room diary. "Mom and Dad spent their honeymoon in this very suite twenty-seven years ago," wrote a just-married Chicago couple. "I hope we can come back for every anniversary."

Rooms for Romance

There are three classifications of rooms at Tickle Pink. Cove-view rooms command tariffs in the lower to upper $100 range, but for just a few dollars more you can have an ocean-view room. Ocean-view suites, the inn's prime accommodations, carry rates from the high $200 range to the mid $400 range. Most rooms have private balconies and about half contain woodburning fireplaces.

Room 6, an ocean-view suite, is decorated in tasteful rose, camel, and cream hues, features a canopied king-sized bed, and has a love seat and chairs set beside the fireplace. The ocean is visible from the sitting area, bedroom, and deck.

Room 23, one of Tickle Pink's largest suites, is decorated in beige and cream tones, and is lavishly furnished with a sectional couch, two televisions, a wet bar, and a king-sized bed from which you'll have a grand water view. In the bathroom is a black tile-trimmed whirlpool tub for two.

Mission Ranch

26270 Dolores Street
Carmel, CA 93923
Telephone: (831) 624-6436

Thirty-one rooms, each with private bath; fifteen with fireplaces and sixteen with oversized tubs. Complimentary continental breakfast served in the ranch's restaurant. Exercise room and tennis courts. Disabled access. Smoking is not permitted. Two-night minimum stay required during weekends; two- or three-night minimum stay required during holiday periods. Moderate to deluxe.

Getting There
From Highway 1 at the Crossroads shopping center, turn west on Rio Road. Turn left on Lasuen Drive (at Carmel Mission) and follow to inn on left.

Mission Ranch

Carmel

*O*riginally a working ranch and dairy farm, this rambling coastal property later became one of Carmel's best-known resorts. Actor-director and local resident Clint Eastwood, who purchased the ranch buildings and several gorgeous acres in 1986 while serving as Carmel's mayor, personally supervised its rehabilitation and reopening. He even hand-picked the handsome country-style wooden beds you'll be sleeping on.

Rooms for Romance

Accommodations at Mission Ranch are not only romantic, they're among Carmel's best bargains. Rates here start at around $100. Of course, the more romantic your room, the higher the price. The sumptuous Meadow View Rooms (low to mid $200 range), for example, have picture windows that frame either the ocean, Point Lobos, or grazing sheep. These are equipped

with king-sized beds, spa tubs, fireplaces, and either patios or decks.

The Hay Loft Bedroom (around $200), housed in an old barn, contains a king-sized bed, potbelly stove, and spa tub, and boasts an ocean view.

Built in 1852, the Bunkhouse is the ranch's oldest structure. Now completely restored, the Bunkhouse (upper $200 range) holds a separate living room, dining room, and bedroom, as well as a kitchen.

The stately farmhouse, which dates from the 1860s, houses six bedrooms (low to mid $100 range) and a cushy parlor.

The Honeymoon Cottage (mid $200 range), restored in 1994, was used as a location in the 1950s movie *A Summer Place*. The sitting room in this romantic retreat has a fireplace.

Mission Ranch also offers a restaurant and a piano bar. The ranch is only one block from Carmel Mission and a half mile from the upscale Barnyard and Crossroads shopping centers.

Bernardus Lodge

415 Carmel Valley Road (P.O. Box 80)
Carmel Valley, CA 93924
Telephone toll-free: (888) 648-9463

Fifty-seven rooms, each with fireplace and tub for
two. Swimming pool, tennis courts, fitness facility,
and health spa. Restaurant. Disabled access.
Smoking is not permitted. Two-night minimum stay
required during weekends. Deluxe.

Getting There
From Highway 1 in Carmel, drive east on Carmel
Valley Road for nine and a half miles. Lodge is on
the left, just beyond the junction of Laureles Grade
and Carmel Valley Road. From Highway 101, take
the Highway 68 south exit and follow highway
toward the Monterey Peninsula. Turn left on
Laureles Grade (also called Highway G20). Lodge is
at the corner of Laureles Grade and Carmel Valley
Road.

Bernardus Lodge

Carmel Valley

*L*est you conclude that all of this region's romantic retreats are clustered at the water's edge, we close our Monterey Bay chapter with a great reason to head to the hills of Carmel Valley. New in 1999, the sumptuous Bernardus Lodge serves up nearly every romantic fantasy imaginable. Luxurious, down-covered king-sized beds, spa tubs for two, woodburning fireplaces, and spa services pamper guests in this glorious coastal mountain setting. There's even a restaurant on site, so there's little reason to stray.

The lodge consists of sumptuous accommodations spread among nine single- and two-story adobe village-style buildings along a terraced hillside. Sharing the grounds are a large swimming pool, two tennis courts, a croquet lawn, a wedding pavilion, and a spa where the ultimate experience is a private room with a couples' shower, oversized treatment tables, and a secluded open-air therapy bath surrounded by a meditation garden. The two of you may even indulge in a skin-smoothing grape seed and red wine scrub or a warm grape seed oil massage.

Rooms for Romance

You'll not be disappointed by any of the accommodations at Bernardus Lodge. The only challenge is choosing among the range of different room types and amenities. They include the lowest priced Garden View Rooms (mid $200 to low $300 range); Premium View Rooms (mid $300 to low $400 range), which have expansive mountain vistas; and Deluxe Jacuzzi Rooms (high $500 to mid $600 range), which offer enclosed outdoor patios with their own spas.

All rooms have king-sized beds, stone fireplaces, and English armoires, and the spacious bathrooms all offer spa tubs for two, separate showers, and double vanities.

The North Valley to the Sierra

DAYTIME DIVERSIONS

In Sacramento, take a romantic (daytime only) stroll through the lush grounds of the state capitol. Mature trees and gardens abound. Touristy Old Sacramento, with its wood plank sidewalks, cobblestone streets, and dozens of specialty shops, is a great place to spend part of an afternoon. You can walk from here to Sacramento's impressive Downtown Plaza shopping mall.

Visitors to Lake Oroville Bed and Breakfast have close access to Bidwell Canyon Marina and its flotilla of rental water craft.

In Murphys, visit the romantic wine caves at Kautz Vineyards, on Six Mile Road, and peaceful Stevenot Winery, a couple of miles out of town near Mercer Cavern off Sheep Ranch Road. Visitors to Moaning Cavern outside Murphys descend a circular staircase into a naturally beautiful subterranean "room" with incredible rock formations. The quaint downtown areas of Grass Valley and Nevada City are chockablock with antique and specialty shops.

In South Lake Tahoe, there's nothing quite like a sunset ride on the aerial tram to the top of Heavenly Valley. Take Ski Run Boulevard from Highway 50 up the mountain to Heavenly Valley. Taking Ski Run Boulevard toward the lake will bring you to the berth of the *Tahoe Queen*, a paddlewheeler with a glass-bottom viewing area. Another sternwheeler, the *M.S. Dixie*, plies the emerald lake from Zephyr Cove Marina on Highway 50 on the Nevada side of the lake.

At the top of the tram in Squaw Valley, the two of you can ice skate twelve months a year. There are bike rentals at Richardson's Resort a couple of miles north of South Lake Tahoe on Highway 89.

TABLES FOR TWO

Within an easy drive of Lake Oroville Bed and Breakfast (see listing in this section) is Lake Madrone restaurant (3 Lakeside Drive) in Berry Creek. Sacramento visitors will enjoy Biba (2801 Capitol Avenue) and Chanterelle at the Sterling Hotel (1300 H Street).

Visitors to Nevada City will enjoy New Moon Cafe (203 York Street), which offers bistro cooking with a French flair. In remote Sierra City, the restaurant pickings are slim; however, try Carlo's Ristorante at the Busch & Heringlake Country Inn (see listing in this section) or the Sierra Buttes Inn (Highway 49 at Hayes Road).

In South Lake Tahoe, we recommend the Fresh Ketch (Tahoe Keys Marina) and Nephele's (1169 Ski Run Boulevard). The Beacon (on the beach at Camp Richardson just off Highway 89) is our favorite place to enjoy a cold beverage with a magnificent lake view.

Amber House Bed-and-Breakfast Inn

1315 Twenty-second Street
Sacramento, CA 95816
Telephone: (916) 444-8085 or
toll-free: (800) 755-6526

Fourteen rooms, each with private bath, telephone, television, and videocassette player; eleven with spa tubs for two. Complimentary bicycle rental for guests. Complimentary full breakfast served at communal table, tables for two, or in your room. No disabled access. Smoking is not permitted. Moderate to deluxe.

Getting There
From Interstate 5 in Sacramento, exit at J Street and drive through town to Twenty-second Street. Turn right and drive three-and-a-half blocks to inn, between Capitol Avenue and N Street. The inn is eight blocks from the state capitol.

Amber House Bed-and-Breakfast Inn

Sacramento

We're the first to admit that California's capital city doesn't come immediately to mind as a logical romantic getaway destination, but we continue to discover sumptuous destinations here that have definite appeal.

Sacramento's charming, tree-shaded midtown area, which has been enjoying a renaissance of late, is the setting for Amber House Bed-and-Breakfast Inn, expanded in recent years to include three different graceful older homes offering visitors a variety of deluxe romantic accommodations.

Amber House is situated eight blocks from the state Capitol and convention center. A number of outstanding restaurants are within walking distance, as is historic Sutter's Fort.

Rooms for Romance

Poet's Refuge is a Craftsman-style home with intriguing vintage features such as a boxed-beam ceiling, hardwood floors, and a clinker-brick fireplace. One of the most romantic rooms here is Lord Byron (upper $100 range), where an oval spa tub presides over a gorgeous bathroom of pink Italian marble.

Longfellow (upper $100 range) also has a romantic bathroom with an oval-shaped spa tub for two.

Next door is our personal favorite, the Artist's Retreat, a restored 1913 Mediterranean-style home. Renoir (mid $200 range) is a mini-suite with a king-sized bed and wrought iron canopy. In the marbled bathroom is a spa tub for two and separate shower. The Van Gogh Room (mid

$200 range) has an awesome solarium bathroom with a wall and a ceiling of glass and a heart-shaped spa tub for two.

Degas has a queen-sized canopied bed and a beautiful bathroom with peach-toned marble, a spa tub for two, and a separate shower.

Since our first visit, the Amber House has grown to include a century-old Colonial Revival-style home with five bedrooms, each reflecting a music theme. The Vivaldi and Mozart rooms (mid $200 range) each have spa tubs for two and decks. For romantics on a budget, the Brahms and Bach rooms are offered in the mid $100 range.

Brigadoon Castle

9036 Zogg Mine Road (P.O. Box 324)
Igo, CA 96046
Telephone: (530) 396-2784 or
toll-free: (888) 343-2836

Five rooms, each with private bath. Complimentary
full breakfast served at communal table. Dinner
served Friday, Saturday, and Sunday night (included
in rates). Spa. No disabled access. Smoking is not
permitted. No minimum stay required. Expensive to
deluxe.

Getting There
From Interstate 5, take the Redding 299 West exit
and follow into Redding. Follow Eureka/299 west
through town. At the Buena Ventura intersection
stop light, turn left and follow one mile to the next
intersection at Placer Road. Turn right on Placer
Road and follow for nine miles to the village of Igo;
go straight at the three-way stop sign in Igo.
Continue following this road (South Fork Road) for

one-quarter mile and take the first right onto Zogg
Mine Road. Follow this road as it winds up the
mountain for just over four miles. Gate entry to inn
on left has a dragon's head and two gargoyles.

Brigadoon Castle

Igo, CA

ver since we began our romantic travels around Northern California, we've been searching for a destination to draw couples to the Trinity Alps region. We finally struck gold with the discovery of the aptly named Brigadoon Castle hidden in the lush hills not far from Redding. Traveling romantics who have sampled the wine country, Pacific coast, and Sierra and who are looking for a change of scene will love this remote hideaway in the northern reaches of the state.

This one-of-a-kind Elizabethan-style manor, built by a Redding physician in the early eighties, offers all the regal fantasy of a castle without the dampness, draftiness, and coldness of a real medieval fortress.

The outdoor areas are equally inviting. There are manicured lawns, patios, walkways, and a goldfish pond. Climb one of the brick staircases to the top of a bluff and relax in the inn's canyon-view hot tub. Dinners are served at Brigadoon on Friday, Saturday, and Sunday evenings.

Rooms for Romance

Room rates noted below are weekend prices that include dinner for two. Midweek rates are lower.

A circular staircase whose railing was carved from a single piece of oak winds to the lovely upper-level bedchambers. Each has its own bathroom trimmed with Italian marble.

For the most authentic castle-like experience, we suggest a night or two in Tyler's Tree Top Room (high $100 range), which occupies two levels. A staircase connects the lower-level sitting room with an enchanting bedroom at the top of the tower, with narrow arrow port windows illuminating a built-in king-sized bed.

Another good choice is Feona's Suite (mid $200 range), whose centerpiece is an inviting white, queen-sized, four-poster bed. A corner sitting area with two cushy chairs looks out over the forest and the distant South Fork Mountain. A bonus is the steam spa in the bathroom.

The Bonny Jean Room (high $100 range) has a balcony overlooking the gardens and forest, while the Swan Room (high $100 range) contains a stained glass window and a carved replica of a bed from the home of author Mark Twain.

In our opinion, the most romantic accommodation is Brigadoon's freestanding cottage (around $300), a two-story retreat with a faux stone facade and European and Scandinavian detailing. Inside is a handsome sitting area with a couch and a gas log stove set on a large brick hearth, a kitchenette, and a deck with a private hot tub. The queen-sized bed is placed in a wood-beamed loft with skylights for stargazing.

The inn is approximately three-and-a-half hours by car from San Francisco, via Interstate 5. Make sure that you leave work a couple of hours early on Friday, casually letting your colleagues know you'll be dining that evening at Brigadoon.

Dunbar House, 1880

271 Jones Street
Murphys, CA 95247
Telephone: (209) 728-2897 or
toll-free: (800) 692-6006

Four rooms, each with private bath, telephone, gas stove, refrigerator with complimentary bottle of wine, and television with videocassette player; one room with spa tub for two. Complimentary full breakfast served at a communal table, in the rose garden, or in your room. Complimentary afternoon refreshments. No disabled access. Smoking is not permitted. Two-night minimum stay required during weekends; three-night minimum stay required during holiday periods. Moderate to expensive.

Getting There
From Highway 4 in Angels Camp, drive eight miles east to Murphys. Turn left on Main Street; then left on Jones, and follow to inn on left. From Murphys Grade Road in Angels Camp, drive eight miles east to Murphys. Turn right on Main Street and drive through town to Jones Street. Turn right on Jones Street to inn on right.

Dunbar House, 1880

Murphys

In our romantic opinion, Murphys is to the Gold Country what Carmel is to the Central Coast. Although it's off the beaten track—and possibly because of it—this charming burg keeps calling us back.

Unlike many Mother Lode towns that have traded their original identities for fast food joints, trailer parks, and modern industry, Murphys is still squarely grounded in the mid 1800s. On Main Street, old-fashioned raised walkways pass under balconied false-fronted shops sell-

ing wares from antiques to dry goods. Hollywood filmmakers, drawn by the town's authentic western look, are frequent visitors.

While many folks come for a day, we suggest spending at least a night or two to truly savor the atmosphere. And there's no better romantic retreat than Dunbar House, 1880, an Italianate mansion separated from Main Street by mature trees and a pretty field where horses graze.

Built over a century ago by State Assemblyman Willis Dunbar for his new bride, Ellen, the inn sits at the edge of a fine old neighborhood. The loving care that innkeepers Barbara and Bob Costa have lavished on the historic home is extended to their guests, who are treated to candlelit breakfasts and comfortable and nicely furnished guestrooms complete with Scandinavian gas stoves. There's even an equestrian taxi service in town that will pick you up at the inn in a carriage.

Rooms for Romance

Dunbar House holds four guest rooms, each with antique furnishings and a gas stove. The two downstairs accommodations are Cedar and Sequoia. Cedar (upper $100 range) is the largest and most expensive, offering an outside porch for a private breakfast in the garden, as well as a spa tub for two. Sequoia (mid $100 range) has a vintage clawfoot tub placed under a window near the gas stove in the bedroom.

Upstairs is the original master bedroom, now called Ponderosa (mid $100 range), from which guests can view the horses across the street and the inn's historic rose garden. The bedroom is accented with Battenburg lace and the bathroom holds a clawfoot tub-and-shower combination.

The spacious second-floor Sugar Pine Suite (upper $100 range) has a queen-sized bed, a sitting room, a CD player, and a private balcony up in the trees. A large bathroom contains a six-foot clawfoot tub and separate shower.

MURPHY'S INN

318 Neal Street
Grass Valley, CA 95945
Telephone: (916) 273-6873 or
toll-free: (800) 895-2488

Eight rooms, each with private bath; four have fireplaces. Complimentary full breakfast served at communal table. No disabled access. Smoking is not
permitted. Two-night minimum stay required during
weekends from April through December and during
holiday periods. Moderate.

Getting There
From eastbound Interstate 80 in Auburn, turn left at
the Highway 49/Grass Valley/Nevada City exit and
drive approximately twenty miles to Grass Valley.
Take the Highway 174/Colfax exit, turn left on
South Auburn Street, and turn left at the second
light on Neal Street to inn on the right. Driving
time to Grass Valley from Sacramento is approximately one hour.

Murphy's Inn

Grass Valley

*O*ne of Grass Valley's most cherished landmarks, this Victorian beauty has deep romantic roots. Built over a century ago by mining magnate Edward Coleman, the home was given as a wedding present to his betrothed.

Now operating as an inn, the graceful home, with its grand veranda and formal parlors, still reflects the opulent lifestyle of its Gold Rush-era builders. Since our first visit, bedrooms have been repainted or wallpapered and recarpeted, and some of the bathrooms have been updated.

Rooms for Romance

Theodosia's Suite (mid $100 range) on the first floor is the largest and plushest room in the main house. A king-sized four-poster bed covered with a floral comforter provides a vantage point for enjoying both a gas fireplace and veranda. Decorated in yellow hues, the suite, originally the home's formal parlor, is furnished with antique chairs and mirrors and old-fashioned knick-knacks. The tiled bathroom has a double shower.

Also on the first floor is the Sequoia Room (low $100 range), extending off the kitchen with a private entry. This cozy step-down room is covered with green carpet and is equipped with a queen-sized bed and a gas stove on a stone hearth. The bathroom is equipped with a large shower. A marble sink from the old days features separate hot and cold spigots.

Murphy's Inn also includes Donation Day House across the street. Sara's Suite (mid $100 range for four people) has a king-sized bed, a separate living room, a fireplace, a kitchen, and a private entry. The other room here is Hanson Suite (mid $100 range), which holds a queen-sized bed, a sitting room with a trundle, and a gas fireplace.

Guests interested in exploring Grass Valley's historic district needn't bother searching for a parking space. The inn is just a short stroll away.

Flume's End Bed-and-Breakfast Inn

317 South Pine Street
Nevada City, CA 95959
Telephone: (916) 265-9665

Six rooms, each with private bath (one room with
detached bath). Complimentary full breakfast served
at tables for two or four. Complimentary snacks and
beverages available day and night. No handicapped
access. Smoking is not permitted. Two-night minimum stay required during weekends and holiday
periods. Moderate.

Getting There

From eastbound Interstate 80 in Auburn, turn left at
the Highway 49/Grass Valley/Nevada City exit and
drive approximately twenty miles to the Broad
Street exit in Nevada City. Drive through town on
Broad Street and turn left on South Pine, across
Spring Street, and across the little bridge to inn.
Driving time to Nevada City from Sacramento is
approximately one hour.

Flume's End Bed-and-Breakfast Inn

Nevada City

*O*ne of the Gold Country's most unusual inns, Flume's End draws its name from a flume that brought Sierra water to a quartz mill that originally occupied this site during the mid-nineteenth century. The mill is gone but the flume still presides over the property. Picturesque Gold Run Creek, which flows next to the inn, provides guests with soothing sounds, especially during the summer months when windows are open and the patio and decks can be savored.

The multilevel Victorian-style inn, built next to the flume against the side of a fairly steep canyon, is full of intriguing staircases, passageways, bays, gables, and windows.

After serving as a residence during the mid-to-late nineteenth century, the inn housed a not-

so-discreet brothel for many years; a secret door for hasty getaways still exists. (Ask about the resident "lost harlot" ghost.)

Proprietors Steve Wilson, a one-time high school teacher, and Terrianne Straw, formerly a vocational rehabilitation administrator, are assisted by Terrianne's gentle golden retriever guide dog.

Rooms for Romance

The bright, bay-windowed Master Bedroom (mid $100 range) holds a queen-sized bed and a spacious bathroom with a spa tub for two, double sinks, and a shower. A private deck overlooks the creek.

The Creekside and Garden rooms (low $100 range) are reached by a narrow wrought-iron spiral staircase. Garden, equipped with a double bed, has a spa tub-and-shower combination and a private deck over the creek. Creekside features a queen-sized bed and boasts a private deck with the best waterfall view. These two rooms share a lower-level sitting area with a gas fireplace, a wet bar, and a television.

High up under the eaves is the Penthouse (low $100 range), which offers a bird's eye view of the main deck and creek. The bathroom here has a clawfoot tub and pedestal sink.

The rustic Cottage (low to mid $100 range) includes a kitchenette, a woodburning stove, a queen-sized four-poster bed, a love seat and chairs, and a bathroom with a tub-and-shower combination. A private secluded deck overlooks trees and waterfalls.

We don't recommend the Stained Glass Room, whose detached bath is situated an inconvenient distance from the room.

Busch & Heringlake Country Inn

Highway 49
Sierra City, CA 96125
Telephone: (916) 862-1501

Four rooms, each with private bath; two rooms with spa tubs for two. Continental breakfast served in the inn's restaurant. Snowshoe packages offered during winter months; golfing and biking tours may be arranged. Disabled access. Smoking is not permitted. Two-night minimum stay required during weekends. Moderate.

Getting There

From eastbound Interstate 80 in Auburn, turn left at the Highway 49/Grass Valley/Nevada City exit and drive approximately twenty miles to Nevada City. Take the Downieville exit and follow toward Downieville for approximately sixty miles to Sierra City and inn on left.

Busch & Heringlake Country Inn

Sierra City

We waited years for some incurable romantic to create a soul-stirring hideaway in this remote little mountain burg. We were just about to give up hope when we received a letter from the Busch & Heringlake Country Inn. Our wait was over.

The most isolated of our romantic north state hideaways, the Busch & Heringlake is a comfortable two-story brick building whose function over the past century has ranged from Wells Fargo stage stop to general store. Proprietor Carlo Giuffre, a former investment banker, bought the place in the mid-1980s and renovated it by hand, creating four modern guest rooms on the second level and a cafe on the ground floor. The hospitable innkeeper, who lives above the inn, runs a relaxed, laid-back operation. Clocks run a little slower up here in the mountains.

Rooms for Romance

We recommend the Phoenix and Young America rooms for romantic getaways. Phoenix (mid $100 range) is a sunny corner room facing the road, and is the only room with a fireplace. It also has a small sitting area, a queen-sized bed, and a private bath with a spa tub for two.

A pink whirlpool tub for two and an adjacent open shower occupy one corner of the Young America Room (mid $100). This room, which has a view of the lush hillside out back, is furnished with a queen-sized brass bed.

Marguerite's Room, a fairly standard room (low $100 range), holds a queen-sized bed and a private bath with a double-spigot shower. The rustically decorated Lusk Meadows (low $100 range) has a queen-sized bed.

Lake Oroville Bed and Breakfast

240 Sunday Drive
Berry Creek, CA 95916
Telephone: (916) 589-0700

Six rooms, each with private bath and telephone; five with spa tubs. Amenities include a billiard table, cassette players in all rooms, and complimentary drinks and snacks. Televisions and videocassette players are available on request. Complimentary full breakfast served in dining room. Barbeque facilities. Disabled access. Pets accepted with advance approval. Smoking is not permitted. Moderate.

Getting There
From Highway 70 in Oroville, exit east at Oroville Dam Boulevard (Route 162) and drive 1.7 miles to Olive Highway (Route 162). Turn right and drive thirteen and a half miles around Lake Oroville. Just after the Foreman Creek State Recreation Area sign, turn left on Bell Ranch Road and drive one-and-a-half miles on the gravel road (becomes Sunday

Drive) to inn on right. Oroville is approximately seventy-five miles from Sacramento, one hundred sixty miles from San Francisco, and two hundred miles from San Jose.

Lake Oroville Bed and Breakfast

Berry Creek

*O*ur theory that the best places are sometimes the most difficult to find was validated again with the discovery of this contemporary charmer in rural Butte County. Located about twenty minutes outside Oroville at the end of a mile-and-a-half gravel road, Lake Oroville Bed and Breakfast ranks as one of our most remote romantic destinations.

Commanding incredible water and valley views from a wooded hilltop high above Lake Oroville, the inn was built in 1992 by proprietors Ron and Cheryl Damberger, former Marin County residents. Constructed as an inn—it's not a reconfigured home—Lake Oroville Bed and Breakfast offers solitude and comfort with extremely reasonable rates. At the time of our visit, all rooms were being offered for around $150 or less.

For guests who prefer not to drive to a restaurant for dinner, the inn provides barbeque facilities. The two of you bring the food; the innkeepers will do the rest.

Rooms for Romance

The small but nicely decorated guest rooms face an expansive, wraparound covered porch and have views into the woods or out over the lake. Each room can be accessed either from an interior hallway or from the porch. All rooms except one have cozy bathrooms containing oval-shaped spa tubs that, while not huge, should accommodate two.

Our favorite room, Victorian (mid $100 range), has a million-dollar view of Lake Oroville and a good portion of Northern California through the branches of a majestic old oak tree. (You can see Mt. Diablo on a clear day.) A king-sized bed sits on deep salmon-colored carpeting.

The valley view from Rose Petal (mid $100 range) is equally or more impressive, but it isn't completely private since the window also faces the porch near the inn's entrance. Rose Petal is equipped with mahogany furniture and a king-sized bed.

One of the most oft-requested rooms is Monet (low $100 range), a bright corner with yellow floral wallpaper and a queen-sized bed. Situated next to the cozy communal sunroom, Monet looks out on the oak-studded hillside.

Vine (just over $100) doesn't have a spa tub, but the nice, handicapped-friendly walk-in shower is big enough for both of you.

SORENSEN'S RESORT

14255 Highway 88
Hope Valley, CA 96120
Telephone: (530) 694-2203 or
toll-free: (800) 423-9949

Twenty-nine cabins, all but two with private baths;
seventeen with woodburning stoves or fireplaces.
Complimentary full breakfast served in restaurant to
guests of certain rooms. Restaurant, cross-country
ski center, and wood-fired sauna. Classes, seminars,
hikes, and tours. Limited disabled access. Smoking is
not permitted. Two-night minimum stay required
during weekends; three- or four-night minimum stay
required during holiday periods. Moderate to
deluxe.

Getting There
From Sacramento/Placerville, follow Highway 50
toward South Lake Tahoe. At Meyers, turn right on
Highway 89, drive eleven miles to the Highway
88/89 junction, and turn left on Highway 88. Resort
is one mile on right.

Sorensen's Resort

Hope Valley

hen weekend Tahoe-bound traffic begins to snarl along Highway 50 as far back as Meyers, the smart money turns right (at Highway 89) and heads for Hope Valley. And while the rest of the folks are still crawling toward Stateline, the two of you will be warming your toes in a high Sierra cabin at Sorensen's Resort.

Occupying a heavenly spot along the Carson River in beautiful Hope Valley, about a half-hour away from the South Tahoe casino area, the resort consists of an eclectic mix of older and newer cabins nestled among glistening aspen.

Rooms for Romance

Don't expect the Ritz in the 1930s and 1940s-era cabins; be aware that some of these are basic and rustic, and nightly rates for some start at less than $100.

Others, however, like the log-walled Snowshoe, Sheepherder, and Creekside with loft bedroom and kitchen (mid $100 to low $200 range), were added only a few years ago and feature contemporary decor and seductive features.

Among the romantic favorites is Waterfir (mid $100 range), surrounded by aspens and set next to a creek. Inside is a queen-sized brass bed, a full kitchen, and a woodstove with a rock hearth. Rockcreek (high $100 to upper $200 range) is a two-level cabin with a kitchen, dining room, and living room with a couch, and a sleeping loft with a queen-sized bed.

Two of the resort's most popular cabins were once part of Santa's Village, an amusement park in Scotts Valley near Santa Cruz. After the park was abandoned, the cabins were taken apart and transported to Sorensen's, where they've been transformed into luxury hideaways. One of these, the Chapel (mid $100 range to low $200 range), is an old-fashioned log cabin with white chinking and hand-hewn doorways.

The other, called St. Nick's (high $100 range to mid $200 range), retains the enchanting, carved window shutters and flower boxes of the original. However, the cabin now boasts a spa tub for two, a fireplace, a sunny deck, and a bedroom loft reached by a circular staircase. Mr. and Mrs. Santa never had it this good.

With a seven-thousand-foot elevation that attracts winter skiers, Sorensen's offers summer activities that include hiking, fishing, and bicycling. The resort also sponsors numerous special programs each year related to hobbies, the arts, cooking, and recreation.

THE TAHOE SEASONS RESORT

3901 Saddle Road
South Lake Tahoe, CA 96157
Telephone: (530) 541-6700 or
toll-free: (800) 540-4874

One hundred sixty rooms, each with private bath
and tub for two; most with fireplaces, videocassette
players, refrigerators, and wet bars. Swimming pool,
spa, tennis courts, valet parking, restaurant, and
lounge. Disabled access. Smoking is allowed.
Moderate to deluxe.

Getting There
From Highway 50 in South Lake Tahoe, take Ski
Run Boulevard (away from the lake), follow to
Needle Peak Road, and turn left. Turn right on
Wildwood Road and left on Saddle Road. From
Sacramento/Placerville via Highway 50, avoid the
often heavy South Tahoe-bound traffic by turning
right on Pioneer Trail just past Meyers and follow-
ing to Ski Run Boulevard. Turn right and follow
directions above from Ski Run Boulevard.

The Tahoe Seasons Resort

South Lake Tahoe

A cozy little inn on the lake it's not. With one hundred sixty rooms, it's the largest of our north state destinations, and from the outside, the multistoried building is fairly nondescript. What's more, a location across the street from Heavenly Valley affords no views of the lake.

If you're wondering what makes The Tahoe Seasons Resort deserving of a spot among our listing of romantic getaways, step inside one of the spacious suites. The rooms here are some of the most intimate we've found in the Tahoe region.

Rooms for Romance

Constructed more than a decade ago, before romance began to figure into the design of most hotels, inns, and resorts, the Tahoe Seasons was ahead of its time. Accommodations (all are larger than five hundred square feet) consist of one-bedroom suites (mid to upper $100 range), each featuring a romantic spa tub for two set between the bedroom and living areas. Hinged privacy screens around the tub open to the living area for a view of the fireplace. A vanity/sink area is adjacent, and the toilet is behind a door.

In addition to queen-sized beds, the suites hold couches, televisions with videocassette players, and small wet bars with microwave ovens. Most have fireplaces. Larger master suites, which can accommodate up to six people, carry rates in the low $200 range.

Set up much like a hotel, Tahoe Seasons has a large, comfortable lounge area on the first floor, as well as a restaurant and bar. Room service is also available. Tennis courts are located

on the roof, and a swimming pool and spa are also available on site. At the time of our visit, the resort offered year-round romance packages with champagne and chocolate.

THE CHRISTIANIA INN

3819 Saddle Road
South Lake Tahoe, CA 96151
Telephone: (530) 544-7337

Six rooms, each with private bath; four with fireplaces. Complimentary continental breakfast delivered
to your room. Restaurant and lounge. No disabled
access. Smoking is not permitted. Two-night minimum stay required during weekends and holiday
periods. Moderate to expensive.

Getting There
From Highway 50 in South Lake Tahoe, take Ski Run
Boulevard (away from the lake), follow to Needle
Peak Road, and turn left. Turn right on Wildwood
Road and left on Saddle Road. Drive two blocks to
inn on left. From Sacramento/Placerville via
Highway 50, avoid the often heavy South Tahoe-
bound traffic by turning right on Pioneer Trail just
past Meyers and following to Wildwood Avenue.
Turn right on Wildwood and left on Saddle Road.
Inn is on the left.

The Christiania Inn

South Lake Tahoe

*I*n a community characterized by cheesy motels that cater to the casino crowd, the Christiania Inn offers travelers a romantic overnight experience that's unfortunately difficult to duplicate in the Lake Tahoe region.

Known affectionately as the "Chris" by those familiar with its charms, the inn tempts visitors with a half-dozen Swiss country-style rooms set behind a Tyrolean-style facade that faces the slopes of Heavenly Valley.

Rooms for Romance

Three two-story suites (upper $100 range) are the inn's premier romantic accommodations. Suite 4, overlooking Heavenly Valley's famous Gunbarrel run, has a dramatic living area with soaring windows, a woodburning fireplace, and a couch. The loft holds a queen-sized bed under mirrors.

In Suite 5, the lower level has a sitting parlor, a wet bar, a dry sauna, and bathroom. A bedroom with king-sized bed and a living room with a fireplace and a love seat are situated on the upper level.

Suite 6, the other two-story retreat, has a living room with a fireplace on a wood-paneled wall and a king-sized bed. There's also a downstairs living room, a wet bar, and a dry sauna. The bathroom has a one-person spa tub.

Suite 3 (upper $100 range) is decorated in Victorian style and features a wet bar and a living area with a cushy couch set into an arched and windowed nook. A fireplace flickers nearby, and a king-sized bed sits in the adjacent bed chamber.

Room 2, also facing Heavenly Valley, is a small room with a bay-windowed nook holding a tiny table with chairs. Room 1 is the inn's least romantic. At the time of our visit, Rooms 1 and 2 were being offered for less than $100.

The impressive rock fireplaces in the downstairs restaurant and bar create an inviting romantic ambience for after-hours dining and cuddling. When making a dinner reservation, ask for table nine, our romantic favorite, situated next to the fireplace.

Because the inn offers no outdoor living areas, the Christiania is, in our opinion, most ideally suited to winter getaways. The ski lifts of Heavenly Valley are within walking distance. The inn does not offer lake views.

Shore House at Lake Tahoe

7170 North Lake Tahoe Boulevard (P.O. Box 499)
Tahoe Vista, CA 96148
Telephone: (530) 546-7270 or
toll-free: (800) 207-5160

Nine rooms, each with private bath and gas fireplace. Complimentary full breakfast served at tables
for two or four in the lakefront dining room. Spa.
No disabled access. Two-night minimum stay
required during weekends. Three-night minimum
stay during holiday periods. Expensive to deluxe.

Getting There
From Interstate 80, exit at Highway 267 in Truckee
and drive south to Lake Tahoe. Turn right on
Highway 28 at Lake Tahoe (also called North Lake
Boulevard) and drive three-quarters of a mile to inn
on left.

Shore House at Lake Tahoe

Tahoe Vista

A lakeview hot tub, a fireplace and a tub for two in your room, breakfast by an award-winning chef, and Lake Tahoe lapping just yards away. . . Regardless of the season, a weekend in the high Sierra couldn't be more romantic.

Our only north shore destination, Shore House at Lake Tahoe is larger than a typical bed-and-breakfast inn and smaller than a hotel, while combining the best features of both. It's one of the area's most impressive lodging options, offering private entries, balconies, decks, gardens, lawns, and an adjoining sandy beach. Owners Barb and Marty Cohen, Lake Tahoe residents for more than 25 years, are troves of helpful information and tips about how to best enjoy the region.

Rooms for Romance

Romantics who like their privacy will savor the Honeymoon Cottage, a remote and cozy hideaway with a vaulted ceiling and furnished with a custom-made, queen-sized log bed, a fireplace, and a spa tub for two and a shower. The cottage also offers a panoramic view of the lake. Another separate cabin called the Studio has a corner gas fireplace, a queen-sized log bed, and a view of the gardens and the lake.

The spacious Moon Room, which boasts a painted ceiling depicting a starry sky, has a king-sized log bed and a large bathroom with a raised spa tub and double tiled sinks.

An awe-inspiring view of Lake Tahoe awaits guests of the Lakeview Room. Located just off the inn's upper terrace, this room has a king-sized log bed placed next to a fireplace. Rainbow trout "swim" on the walls of the pretty tiled bathroom, which has a shower.

Located on the ground floor and one of the inn's larger rooms, the Pine Room offers a king-sized log bed and a pine-paneled bathroom with an oversized tub and shower.

Rates at Shore House range from the mid $100 range to the mid $200 range depending on the time of year. The inn is open year-round.

Appendix

More Travel Resources for Incurable Romantics

Weekends for Two in Northern California: 50 Romantic Getaways
(The original romantic travel guide, revised and updated)

Weekends for Two in Southern California: 50 Romantic Getaways
(Intimate destinations from the Santa Barbara coast to the sultry desert)

Weekends for Two in the Pacific Northwest: 50 Romantic Getaways
(Coastal, mountain, and island hideaways in Oregon, Washington, and British Columbia)

Weekends for Two in New England: 50 Romantic Getaways
(Maine, Vermont, New Hampshire, Massachusetts, Connecticut, and Rhode Island)

Weekends for Two in the Middle Atlantic States: 50 Romantic Getaways
(Virginia, Maryland, Washington, D.C., New Jersey, Pennsylvania, and New York)

Weekends for Two in the Southwest: 50 Romantic Getaways
(Arizona, New Mexico, and the Four Corners Region)

With more than 150 color photos in each book, these are the definitive travel guides to the nation's most romantic destinations. All published by Chronicle Books, these editions are available from your local bookstore or from on-line booksellers.

Free Travel Update
We continue to discover new romantic destinations and reevaluate our currently featured inns and small hotels, and are happy to share this information with readers. For a free update on our new discoveries and recommendations and new books in the *Weekends for Two* series, please send a stamped, self-addressed business-sized envelope to Bill Gleeson, Weekends for Two Update, P.O. Box 6324, Folsom, CA 95763, or contact us via e-mail at weekends42@aol.com. You may also keep up-to-date on new releases by visiting the Chronicle Books web site at www.chroniclebooks.com.

Index

Cast Your Vote!

Northern California's Most Romantic Hotel or Inn

Complete and mail to Bill Gleeson, *Weekends for Two in Northern California*, Chronicle Books, 85 Second Street, San Francisco, California, 94105. We'll share your favorites in future editions.

Our favorite Northern California romantic retreat is:

_____

Name of hotel/inn

_____

City/Town

What makes this place special?

_____

_____

_____

Your name/address (optional)

_____

_____